Original SWILL

1981 - 2001

Neil Williams

Vile Fen Press

a division of Klatha Entertainment an Uldune Media company

i

Williams, Neil, 1958-
(Jamieson-Williams, Neil, 1958-)

    Original SWILL 1981 - 2001 / Neil Williams.

ISBN 978-1-894602-27-3
    1. Science fiction--History and criticism.

2. Science fiction fans. I. Title.

Published by Vile Fen Press
an imprint of Uldune Media
504 – 635 Canterbury Street,
Woodstock, ON, Canada, L4S 8X9.
www.uldunemedia.ca

Table of Contents

An Introduction: On SWILL

Neil Williams

In the beginning... Uh, no!

Once upon a time... Uh-uh. Scrap!

A long, long time ago. Way back, in the palaeodigital era. When the only mobile phones were the DynaTAC "bricks" that had no internet, no apps, could only do voice calls, and were super expensive. When to make a phone call from Toronto to Vancouver during business hours (9 AM to 5 PM) would cost you $10.00 per minute. Back when most people didn't own videorecorders and if you wanted to watch a programme on television you HAD to watch it when it aired at its scheduled time and date. When people still used electric typewriters and when the Internet looked as interesting as Notepad. That is when SWILL was born.

The actual origin story of SWILL has been pieced together over the past decade. It was initially a "lark" that became semi-serious. It began as a surreal joke; distributing a convention boycott flyer at the convention to be boycotted itself. That was supposed to end with the publication of the first issue. SWILL was intended as a one-shot. However, the reaction we received from the "movers and shakers" of Toronto science fiction fandom at the time, spurred further issues. SWILL pissed off the Big Name Fans in Toronto, especially those involved in fanzines and in running science fiction conventions. And we revelled in their anger, as we were all in our very early 20s. It can be amusing watching forty year-olds explode and fume...

WARNING: Issues #1 though #6.5 were written forty years ago and within the context of that time period. Many

politically incorrect statements will be contained
within these issues. However, the entire intention of
SWILL was to be offensive. It was kind of the print
fanzine version of a radio "shock jock"; intending to
be provocative or irreverent and offensive to much of
the specific audience, science fiction fandom.
Sometimes we made some points, other times we were just
offensive. SWILL has always been an acquired taste.

This is the first volume in a collection of SWILL
issues that spans decades (okay, not the 1990s -- I was
too busy being a parent back then...). This first
volume, Original SWILL presents the original issues
from 1981, the 1984-1986 issues of Daughter of SWILL
Mother of Scum, and the 2001 SWILL Online.

Enjoy))

Neil Williams
August, 2024

TRIGGER WARNING

SWILL is written to BE OFFENSIVE. It was written to offend back forty years ago. It was not written for the sensibilities of the mid 2020s. If you are someone who becomes so very traumatised that you have to curl up into a ball in bed for a week, after watching an episode of Friends where Chandler Bing talks about his father. If you find the 1990s sitcom Friends too racist, sexist, homophobic, and transphobic and believe that it should never be permitted to air again and that all of the recordings and mastertapes of this series MUST be destroyed so there is now no danger that you will ever encounter this television show ever in the future; then SWILL is definitely not for you.

SWILL is offensive to many (including and not limited to):
- Trufen
- mediafen
- reptilophiles
- comic book retailers
- used book retailers
- comic book fans
- capitalist swine
- toad-spawn
- Christian fundamentalist fascists
- masturbatory satanic vegetarians
- LGBT people
- mentally challenged people
- body image challenged people
- body image challenged Trekkies
- just to name a few...

You have been warned.

The Maplecon Slandersheet: How it all Began

This was bashed out on my old manual typewriter a few days before Lester Rainsford and I went to attend Maplecon III in Ottawa, Ontario. Ed was staying with our mutual friend, Andrew Hoyt, who lived and was doing his post-grad in Ottawa. I was staying with a female friend I had met at last year's convention. With the passage of time and evidence from photos and other people's recollections I can now state with a high degree of confidence that I attended both Maplecon II in 1979 and Maplecon III in 1980. By 2001, I had in my memory mushed both Maplecons into one single Maplecon in 1980. Maplecon II in 1979 was the Maplecon where the Droogs won best group costume and Maplecon III in 1980 was when the Slandersheet was distributed.

Although there was a comic book fan presence at Maplecon II, it was a major part of Maplecon III and was prominent in their pre-convention promotion. Lester was uncertain about attending a comic book convention pretending to be a science fiction convention. But plans had already been made.

Thus, the boycott flyer was born. It was a freeform rant about comic books and comic book fans having no place at a science fiction convention. It was offensive and crude and was signed by OSFiC (the major Toronto-based science fiction club at that time). It was surreal in that the only way one would receive the flyer is by attending the convention the flyer is calling you to boycott.

At the convention, we set out some piles of flyers. Then went off to participate in the convention. I went to renew the flyers and was happy to see they were all

gone, and put out more. I went to the washroom and
when I returned all the flyers were gone. I put out a
smaller amount. Then came back five minutes later, no
flyers. Then I put out only five flyers and found a
seat nearby. Sure enough, someone came by and took
them all; that person was wearing a Convention
Committee badge. I went and told Lester and Andrew and
then the fun began. We placed small piles of flyers in
the panel rooms, in the dealers' room, at the hotel
bar. I borrowed some scotch tape and we started
putting flyers up in the washroom stalls, by the
elevators, in the elevators, on the walls in the
convention space. We continued to put them up on the
flyer table, one flyer at a time, until the Convention
Committee stationed a convention security person at the
flyer table. We got rid of the remaining flyers, and I
went up to the Hospitality Suite to rendezvous with my
girlfriend and Lester and Andrew went for some food and
then headed back the Andrew's place.

I really didn't attend the convention much on the
Saturday. My girlfriend and I attended the costume
judging and the dance that followed, then we returned
to her place. On Sunday, we went out for brunch, I
kissed her goodbye, then went to meet up with Lester,
to head back to Toronto.

And that was it, we thought. Just a silly prank.

What we didn't know at the time at the time, and I
would not discover until decades later, was that there
were divisions within OSFS (the Ottawa Science Fiction
Society), the organisation that ran Maplecon. In part,
the division was typical for the time period, literary
fans vs fans of the genre in other mediums (including
comic books). But, there was the other factors of
those who felt that Maplecon was growing too fast. The
segment within OSFS that supported the comic book
addition to Maplecon actually believed that OSFiC was
the author of the Boycott Flyer. OSFiC was known at

the time to be a staunch supporter of maintaining the
purity of the "precious bodily fluids" of Toronto
literary science fiction fandom from those mediafen.
So there was some logic to that belief by the comic
book segment of OSFS, but only a small bit of logic.

I did hear that the "powers that be" in Toronto fandom
were upset about the Maplecon Slandersheet and that
there would be "hell to pay" when they discovered who
was responsible. And this is why Swill came into
existance.

For now, here is the infamous, horrible, dripping with
evil Maplecon III Slandersheet of 1980...

SUPPORRT SCIENCE FICTION READER'S RIGHTS!   BOYCOTT MAPLECON III!

Every year, true science fiction fans are degraded by the travesty of a 'sf convention' mounted by an incestuous unholy allienace of ottawa peseudo-fans and comic book fanatics. This farce of a money-grubbing grasp for oub monwy is solely designed to enrich the pockets of of stupid slothbrained comic book collectors who use this ill-beggoten gains to buy more of their purelle little picture books with stories for morons who read out INHII.

lud.

Why do true sf fans have to put up with twits who think superman and batshit and the rest of the fucking horde   are up there in litrary merit with EE Smith and Leguin and the rest of the sf greats? Why must true sf fans have to listen to eager beaver dipshit talks about Green Hornet wants to screw Robin??   Or does wonder woman use vibrating tampons???

F urthermore, there is also at this convention a dealers section. These dealers, who sometimes have the idiotic idea that they are sf 'fans', are really one of the biggest assholes to screw true sf fans that there is.

Have you ever tried to buy a sude used book? You know what outrageous profiteering prices these leeches charge for even torn copies of Ivor Jorgensons Ten From Infinity? A cocksucker book if there ever was one? Go to Bakka books in Torontso and try to buy a copy of niven's Shape of space. Just try to. Why are used books so expensive? Because it is a plot!!! A fucking ploy by assholes who try to get rid of their useless old paperbacks, and want more money!!! These capitalist swine rip-off the true sf fan by denying the true sf fan many old good books. Also, many used sf bookstores run by these leeches sell comic books, thus perpeptuating this swinish breed.

Look, if you are a true sf fan, why dont you leave now and let the rest of the fairies & screw themselves in the ass and jerk off over Green Hornet in heroic poses? Let the bastafd fucking toad-spawn be fed to chickens!! Stnd up for sf rights!!!

Sincerely yours, The Ontario Scince Fiction Association
                                          club
                                          the motherfuckers

SWILL: The Original Period

The first issue of SWILL was to be a oneshot. Lester
and I had heard that there was a hullaballoo about the
Maplecon Slandersheet and decided that we would do a
small fanzine that attacked fandom. I said that I
would bring copies to the next monthly fan gathering at
the end of February. And so the week of the 22nd of
February we cobbled together the first issue of SWILL,
printed about 50 copies that I took to the monthly
"Bas-Con" on February 28th.

Some people hated SWILL with a passion. Others loved
it. Others liked it because the "Old Guard" fumed
about it. I had outed myself as the "one responsible",
but there was no "hell to pay". Just some ostracism.
So what did we do? We wrote and printed more issues.

Now, there was a person had become involved with SWILL
who really wasn't a science fiction fan. He was a
gamer, back in the day when that meant board games, and
he like Traveller, but was more into military strategy
games. He began writing content for us and he created
the "My Fame" comic strip. He also created BeeSwill as
he felt that Swill needed to be more frequent than
monthly (which it was for the first four issues).
BeeSwill may have been inspired by SWILL but it is not
SWILL, nor part of the SWILL lineage. It is an
evolutionary side branch and separate species.

In May, I moved to Vancouver. I intended to continue
SWILL as SWILL East (with Lester in charge) and SWILL
West (run by me). Each SWILL would have shared content
and unique content. Then there was the postal strike
and SWILL ground to a halt.

In August of 1981 I published SWILL #4b (aka SWILL
#4.5), a brief Worldcon Issue. SWILL #5 came out in
September. The final original SWILL issue, #6 was

published and distributed in December of 1981.
Unfortunately, none of the people who wrote content for
it have copies, and I don't have a copy. It is lost...
This was the final original 1981 issue of SWILL.

In 1984, I planned to revive SWILL. I just wasn't sure
how I wanted to do this and what the subject material
would be. I had lost any interest in ticking off
Toronto fandom. Or Vancouver fandom. I just wanted to
deal with some larger issues in the genre. And also
tweak the nose of certain groups within science fiction
fandom. I was working in radio at the time and was
also involved in the Anti-Arms Race movement of the
early 1980s. I was also involved in one of the "grass
roots" organisations involved in Operation Solidarity
which was moving towards a province-wide general strike
against the Social Credit government. I had also just
discovered cyberpunk and Barry Malzberg's "The Engines
of the Night: Science Fiction in the Eighties".

There were three issues of Daughter or Swill, Mother of
Scum. The first issue probably came out in the spring
of 1984 (I had created Black Star productions for my
independent radio content from that produced for CFRO-
FM around May or June of that year). The First
Trimester was a critique of science fiction and fandom
(there is a strong influence of the essays of Malzberg
and a weaker influence of LeGuin) and written as a film
script. Second Trimester was published in June 1985
and is on the subject of there being a "winnable
nuclear war" and that in post global nuclear war world
we will be able to rebuild civilisation. I say no to
both concepts. Third Trimester has been lost. This is
due to the fact that I printed few copies of the zine
and thus sent few out into the world. The subject
matter of this issue was the lack of alien aliens in
science fiction and it was published in 1986. These
have been designated as SWILL #6.5a through to SWILL
#6.5c (because I had forgotten about them when I made
SWILL Online, SWILL #7.

I wrote Scum, but never published it. It has been lost forever.

In 2001, I published SWILL Online. I printed off about 100 copies and a new Boycott flyer (to boycott Ad Astra 2001) and went down to Toronto to attend Ad Astra. This was well received by old friends and not so by old non-friends. SWILL Online was also published online. As of February 2025, the old website still exists (spelling mistakes and all) at

https://members.tripod.com/swill_2001/index.html

SWILL Online is SWILL #7 and the last of issues in the original period of SWILL.

SWILL #1

February 1981

SWILL

VOL. 1

NO. 1

SWILL: a Toronto area disgustzine, or vilezine produced by the Vile Fen
Press, and the unofficial organ of the Vile Fen. Our address is:
Rm. 221, winters college residence, york university, 4700 keele street,
downsview, ontario, canada, m3j 1j9.

EDITORIAL

What is this zine you are probably asking? What is a disgustzine, aside
of being a poor attempt at a pun? Who are the Vile Fen? Really! What
gives you the right to ask these questions. Who do you think I am, Information
Canada? Find out for yourselves. What do you think is inside your head,
potatos? Well, there might be, you never know with some fans. But if you
are one of the privillaged few in fandom that actually possesses some brains
in their skulls, figure it out for yourself; I ain't telling you. So go
fuck yourself.
(screw the capitals,too much of a bother)
this is a unique type of zine. there are many fanzines that are digusting
and obnoxious but usually it's only one article that is so, maybe even an
issue. Usually it is unintentional. well this aint, sucker. we're gonna
be lewd and crude and even downright rude, AND WE DON'T GIVE A SHIT WHAT YOU
THINK. we'll tell it as we see it and we'll publish your comments on what
we have to say. mind you, we most likely'll tear your comments to shreds in
our loc column too.
why are we doing this? because we feel like it dummy. because we think
that a lot of what goes on in fandom is full of shit. Also, there's a lotta
assholes in fandom, as we see it. Everyone thinks he is a truefan, whatever
the fuck that might be. According to this magazine the closest thing there
is to a truefan is the guy who reads science fiction, maybe goes to the odd
convention, but generally leads a normal life. This is the guy the genre
depends on. this is what it's all about. this is the person who actually
reads, he is litterate, he functions in society. i'm not saying that this guy
is a dullard because he probably isn't. But what he also isn't is a misfit,
which a lot of fen are. FIAWOL is not his style, by fannish standards, he's
a mundane. Don't fool yourself fen, he's not a silent minority. In fact,he's
probably a majority. I know many people who read science fiction that have
never joined a sf. club or gone to a convention. the closest thing they do
that could be classed as a fannish activity is write a letter to the
editor of their favourite sf. magazine. so yo're not the majority of the
sf. audience, those who write fanzines, frequently go to cons, dedicate your
life to fandom. nor are any of you truefen, not by my reckoning, for the REAL
truefan is probably at home or on his lunchbreak reading Serpent's Reach or
some other novel and not this zine, for REAL truefen rarely recieves
a fanzine, if ever.

Neil Williams

Editor: Neil Williams
Columnist: Lester Rainsford

Contributers: Steve Vano
                Scrotm the Unbathed

Art by Neil Williams

SWILL: volume 1, number 1, February 1981.

MEDIAFEN SUCK

Not a nice thing to say, but i don't care. Why should I? Mediafen
probably aren't gonna read this article or hear anything about it, unless
someone reads it to them. And that's the point. Mediafen don't read enough,
or if they do read they read comic books. hardly what i call great literature.
Of course i don't consider most of science fiction to be great literature, but
at least the majority of sf. works are superior to harliquen romances and the
usual run-of-the-mill bestseller novels. it is worthwhile reading.

but mediafen don't read. they watch their silly little movies and tely
shows and think that they are sf. fans. Bullshit!!! psuedo-science fans,
space fantasy fans but not science fiction fans. Never!

why is this so? because there are virtually no science fiction films.
i can name but one recent film that can qualify as a science fiction film.
that film is the PBS production of LeGuin's THE LATHE OF HEAVEN. If you go
back, say, fifteen years this number increases to five. (2001, silent running,
a clockwork orange, a boy and his dog, and the lathe of heaven) still,that's
not many films, not enough to justify a large sf media fan following.
Nonetheless, there is a large sf. media fan following. why? because these
morons think that such absolute rubbish as, star wars, close encounters of the
third kind, battlestar galactica, alien, star trek the motion picture, the empire
strikes back, and flash gordon are science fiction. HELP!! at best, they are
entertaining space opera, at worst, they are bad space opera. but science fiction,
YOU GOTTA BE BLODDY KIDDING!!!

But unfortunately, most mediafen don't realise this, or don't accept such
judgements of what they worship. they just revell in the glories of celluloid
garbage quoting lines from Obi-wan Kenobi's speaches as if they came from the
Bible or some other great book. Mr. Spock is their demi-god. Captain kirk
can do no wrong(he doesn't even go to the bathroom). Luke skywalker, who has
the intellect of your average georgia redneck, is a hero to be admired. and
wouldn't it be great to be super-macho like buck rogers and starbuck and get
to show off your john travolta imitation at the galactic roller disco.

FUCK OFF!! you twits make me wantta puke! do we need such insipid
dungheads in fandom? must we cater to their whims at SCIENCE FICTION conventions?
NO, of course not! I agree that there are some science fiction movies and have
nothing against showwing such movies at sf. conventions. I like movies too.
but don't show buck rogers in the 25th century or the black hole at OUR
conventions.

if the mediafen want to show their dipshit little flicks, let them show
them at their own conventions. let them hold their own infantile media crudcons,
where they can babble all they want about how wonderful han solo is, and wonder
whether luke will get to screw that slut of a princess. And maybe, if we're
really lucky, they'll hold their disgusting conventions in cities far, far
away from REAL sf. fans. Baffin island would be a perfect site for a mediacon.
so would mount st. helens.

so don't bow to these scums' demands. Don't show their stupid, obnoxious,
purile shit films at sf. cons. They have no place there or in SCIENCE FICTION
fandom.

Neil Williams

PISSING ON A PILE OF OLD AMAZINGS
....a modest column by Lester Rainsford

Have you noticed what I've noticed lately? No, of course not: few people
are as brilliantly perceptive as I. However, since you have the class,
distinction, erudition, and sheer all-round social competence to be reading
this epistle of uncommon literary grace, let me deign to inform your poor,
benighted, molecularly deprived soul.

Have you ever fucked a dragon before? Are you in the act of fucking
one right now? (For obvious reasons, oral sex is not highly recommended
with a dragon.) Do you have a dragon fetish?

Unless you wear silk panties on your head and bowler hats on your buns
—-in short, unless you are a depraved whacko—-the answer is obviously NO.

So then, why the terrible (literally!) emphasis placed on dragons these
days? Dragons here, dragons there, dragons everywhere! Dragon poop falling
from the skies! And you though it was good that cows don't fly??

The average pb cover will have a....dragon on it. Ah, you ask, what does
a dragon have to do with Foundation and Empire? And this, Gentle Reader, is
my point.

WE ARE IN THE MIDST OF A DRAGON CRAZE!!!! Perpetrated by some dragon-hap-
py morons, no doubt. Go to an 'art' auction at any con (anyone who wonders
why fen art is placed in quotation marks probably thinks Van Gogh is a
fast Econoline), and what do you see? NAKED GIRLS BEING CARRESSED BY NAKED
DRAGONS!!!! That's all. Nothing else. Just hordes of imbecillically-
drawn, faded Technicolour, sex-inspiring (but why???) dragons.

What should we do about this menace?

Charly, we must do something to free dragon-lovers from their pernicious,
obnoxious , anti-social, pro-reptilian, antedeluvian, monarchist, papist,
satanist, fascist, Republican, vegetarian, pavlovian, perverted, disgusting,
deviant, sodomistic, masturbatory, indecent, degenerate, decadent, lesbian,
anal, filthy, messy, and smelly fixation, and put them on the road to
enlightenment, virtue, Godlyness, purity, decencey Catholicism, the Jehova's
Witnesses, EST, hot tubs, warm tubs, cold tubes, apple pie, mother, baseball ,
respect for the family, the glorious Canadian flag, the noble beaver, and
Caledon East.

For your information, Caledon East is a small town on Airport Road, south
of Mono Mills. It is not to be confused with the town of Caledon, which is
a very puny hamlet at the intersection of highways 10 and 81. Furthermore,
the hamlet of Caledon is not to be confused with the Town of Caledon, a
regional municipality occupying the northern half of the regional municipali ty
of Peel. Probably the most interesting and scenic spot in Peel is at the
Forks of the Credit. Here, the sparkling Credit runs beneath the tall cliffs
of the Niagara escarpment. Ice cream is available at a shop close to the
forks.

The Forks of the Credit are accessible from Highway 10: head north and
turn left at the sign. Or, from the north-west, you can travel through
Belfaountain. Be sure to stop at at their old general store, and visit
Belfountain Conservation are,a, complete with a ten-metre artificial water-
fall. If you really know what you're doing, you can get to the Forks from
Inglewood, encountering some spectacular scenery and hair-pin turns on the
way, but this is best left to the locals.

Next column, we will explain how to visit Cheltenham, Erin, Victoria Cross,
Snelgrove, Bolton, Castlemore, and Ebenezir. Although Erin is, of course,
strictly speaking in Dufferin County.

Oh, shit, I forgot to mention Hillsburgh and Grand Vallye, although they're
also in Dufferin County.

FUN AND GAMES

THRASH THE TREKKIE
Romulan Games Research, Inc., Postal Box 1, the Romulan Empire.
40 Page Rulebook—3 Slaves (cost in Terrans or equivalent)
Designed by Romulus and Remus

A role-playing game involving good guys and Terrans. To add to the im-
mediacy of the game, it is played live—not on paper. Perfect for SCA
members (Society for Creative Anarchism). Required: weapons ! (Not
for the trekkies, you Klingon fool!) Almost any sort of weapons will
do: lasers, blasters, field guns, howitzers, killer sattelites, battleships,
the Canadian Armed Farces (both of them), steel files, blow driers, pumpkin
seeds, 1.5 litre pop bottles, dirty socks priests' frocks, Italian farts,
horny Greeks, rubber darts, six-furrow ploughs, high-speed threshers,
subway trains, high-speed planes, M-16's, neutron bombs, panzer tanks,
missle banks, nuclear subs, IRA thugs, Rill food, Ellison books, dirty
looks, short-order cooks, baler twine, What's My Line?, diet food, In
the Mood, and used condoms. Of course most Trekkies are fat and pimply,
so they can't really run very fast, and they tend to burst when struck.
For this reason it is recommended that one do them in, say, by rubbing them
with steel wool until all the fat has been rubbed away. This will usually
leave the trekkie without any head, and the rest of the disgusting mass
can be fed to the slaves.
It is also fun to simpl y run them over with your battlecruiser. This
however loses the personal touch.
A family game, suitable for ten to a thousand players, depending on the
supply of Trekkies!
        —reviewed by Scrotum the Unbathed

    THANKS SCROTUM. another fun game to play is FUN WITH FRITZ. this is the
perfect game for relieving tension. it costs very little and you can play it
anywhere. There are two versions of the game. One requires a stuffed dummy,
which is the fritz and the other requires a masochist, which is the fritz.
Other equiptment required is as follows, willy whacker and bowlerhats(optional)
Willy whackers differ in type depending on the type of fritz you use. if you
use a stuffed fritz a standard real-wood willy whacker, baseball or cricket bat
is required. If you use a live fritz it is suggested that you use hollow plastic
tubes for willy whackers.(standard willy whackers can also be used but they
usually result in things getting kinda messy. The game is played by having 2-10
players adopt the roles of CLOCKWORK ORANGE droogs and tolchock the hell out of
the fritz, beating his head to a pulp, stomping on his yarbbles, kicking his
guts, and ripping him to bits and burning the little pieces and feeding them to
the cat!!!An educational game that's fun for the whole family.
        —reviewed by steve vano and neil williams

******* NEXT PAGE. THE INFAMOUS MAPLECON III SLANDERSHEET!!!! ********

SUPPORRT SCIENCE FICTION READER'S RIGHTS!   BOYCOTT MAPLECON III!

Every year, true science fiction fans are degraded by the travesty of a 'sf convention'
mounted by an incestuous unholy allienace of ottawa peseudo-fans and comic book fanatics.
This farce of a money-grubbing grasp for oub monwy is solely designed to enrich the pockets of of stupid slothbrained comic book collectors who use this ill-beggoten gains to
buy more of their purelle little picture books with stories for morons who read out IXMIM.
lud.

   Why do true sf fans have to put up with twits who think superman and batshit and the rest
of the fucking horde   are up there in litrary merit with EE Smith and Leguin and the
rest of the sf greats? Why must true sf fans have to listen to eager beaver dipshit
talks about Green Hornet wants to screw Robin??   Or does wonder woman use vibrating
tampons???

   F urthermore, there is also at this convention a dealers section. These dealers,
who sometimes have the idiotic idea that they are sf 'fans', are really one of the biggest
assholes to screw true sf fans that there is.

   Have you ever tried to buy a sude used book? You know what outrageous profiteering
prices these leeches charge for even torn copies of Ivor Jorgensons Ten From Infinity?
A cocksucker book if there ever was one? Go to Bakka books in Torontso and try to buy
a copy of niven's Shape of space. Just try to. Why are used books so expensive?
Because it is a plot!!! A fucking ploy by assholes who try to get rid of their useless old
paperbacks, and want more money!!! These capitalist swine rip-off the true sf fan by
denying the true sf fan many old good books. Also, many used sf bookstores run by these
leeches sell comic books, thus perpeptuating this swinish breed.
Look, if you are a true sf fan, why dont you leave now and let the rest of the fairies
& screw themselves in the ass and jerk off over Green Hornet in heroic poses? Let the
bastafd fucking toad-spawn be fed to chickens!! Stnd up for sf rights!!!

                    Sincerely yours, The Ontario Scince Fiction Association
                                                     club
                                                     the motherfuckers

A NOTE ON Letters Of Comment

This is an example of the kind of LOC that we don't want to see and which if we do recieve we won't even bother to print.

Dear Swill,
you're zine is written and edited by disgusting perverts who can't even spell properly. How can you talk about literacy when you spell literate and such easy words as loud wrong. As far as I'm concerned you're all a bunch of morons.

Vladimir Schnerd
Red Army,
Afganistan.

Mr. Schnerd, thank you for being concerned about spelling in this zine. few people are concerned about spelling these days. But it is the editorial opinion that in SWILL our content is more effective if myself and our contributers disregard standard literary and journalistic conventions. concerning you comment that we're all a bunch of morons, please send another letter elaborating on that subject. Ed.

This, now, is an example of the type of letter we really want.

Dear dummies,
How dare you write a zine that attacks fandom. We don't need that type of zine around. It helps give fandom a bad name. there should be laws prohibbiting perverts like you from producing disgusting magazines like Swill!

unsigned

your
I note that you are too cowardly to sign ### name to your letter. oh well, that's your problem. we don't do psycho-analysis here. As for giving fandom a bad name, # i believe that fandom has done an efficant enough job in that area already. concerning your comments about new legistlation. Haven't you heard about freedom of the press, you fascist motherfucker!!!

ENDNOTE

Hope you've enjoyed the first ish of SWILL. If you didn't enjoy it, TOUGH SHIT. Please send all locs to the address listed on page one. Swill costs $1.00 (includes postage) in canada and $1.25 (includes postage) for yankee residents There is no subscription rate, as yet. we'll be back again to give the proverbial finger to fandom in about a month. See you then.

$1.00

SWILL

VOL. 1

NO. 1

SWILL #2

March 1981

SWILL ツ!

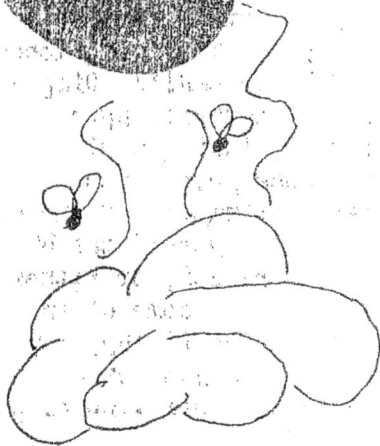

A PILE OF SHIT

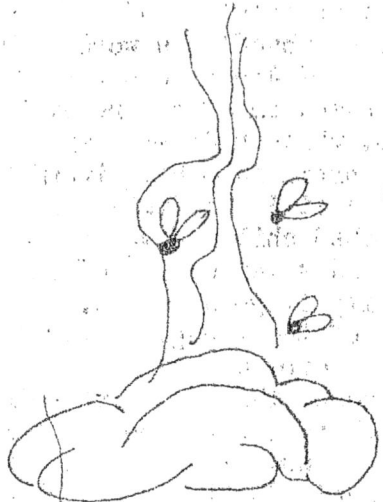

ANOTHER PILE OF SHIT

FANDOM

[PREFERRED BY 8 OUT OF 13 FLIES OVER ORDINARY BRANDS OF SHIT]

VOl 1 No 2

GUEST EDITORIAL

1st Reverand B. Jeramiha Jones
1st Fundamentalist Church of Iowa

Have you ever noticed how much SMUT there is in science fiction?
No! Of course not! That's because you're all godless perverts! That is
why you are not totally repulsed by all those old Amazing and Thrilling Wonder
Stories covers of WOMEN FLYING AROUND IN SPACE IN THEIR UNDERWEAR!!! Disgusting!
Filthy! (And you wonder why Thrilling Wonder Stories was so thrilling.)
Because every pubescent male was JERKING OFF at the covers, that's why!

Smut is rampant in science fiction. Just look at those permiscuous
societies created and the hedonistic, perverse shipboard activities of the crews
in A. B. Chandler's works. Or just look at the Kelly Freas cover of the DAW
edition of James Schmitz's the Lion Game. The heroine is dressed, or rather
undressed, in a most revealing costume, about to be attacked by some alien
beast, which undoubtabley is planning to rape her and stick its filthy, repulsive,
hairy organ into her virginal vagina and commit a wholey, indecent act of
beastiality! And this book is displayed in bookstores in the full view of pure,
untouched children whose clean minds are ripe to be warped.

And science fiction fans wonder why their genre is not respected by the
majority of good, clean, lawbidding citizens. Why? Because it perverts the
minds of the young, polluting their precious bodily fluids! It is filth.
Dung. Garbage. I know, for I have made an extensive study into the effects
of reading this degenerate fiction.

Oh yes, I've been to those hedonistic rituals dalled science fiction
conventions. I have seen the hideous practices of these followers of Satan.
Drinking! Smoking the killer weed! And pre-marital sex abound at these
gatherings of the godless! As these heathens pay homage to their idols, the
science fiction writers. Those parasites whose sole purpose is to corrupt
the minds of wholesome youths with their seditious writings that leads their
inocent victims down the dark path of self masturbation, blindness, and
sticky fingers.

Yea, I have been in their temple of carnal pleasures, the convention suite
where drunkeness and lust rule. Teenagers, and most science fiction fans are,
are turned on to liquor and sex, naked back-rubs, skinny dipping, and wild
orgies. Young twisting bodies writhing on the beer-cap strewn floor.

Yea, I have been there. I have been seduced by wanton, nubile sixteen
year olds. Been dragged into their pagan groping matches. Drunk my fill of
Pan Galactic Gargle Blasters and squirmed with unrightous delight and softly
moaned as the cigarette butts burned holes deliciously into my flesh. Cracked
the whip over the prone bodies of demonic sinners with urgent anticipation,
passion filling me with each strike.

Yea, I have dwelt in the den of science fiction smut, witnessed the dark
depravity of fandom. I have fucked, blown, committed acts of sodomy and
beastiality that I may educate you on the utter filth of science fiction and its
semen covered hordes which I have attempted to save from the dance of Satan.

Editor: Neil Williams   Contributers: Rev. B. J. Jones,
Columnist: Lester Rainsford   J. Goobly, P. Leninski
                    Art: Stephano, N. Williams

SWILL: volume 1, nubmer 2, March 1981.   © 1981 Vile Fen Press
35 High Park Ave., #1906, Toronto, Ontario, Canada.

FEN "ART"?

Have you ever been to a science fiction convention art show? If you haven't, consider your eyes lucky. If you have, don't whine to me. If I can take it so can you. But for the benifit of those persons who've been fortunate enough not to have seen fen "art" a quick tour of what you'll find in your average con art show. Dozens of poorly drawn, ineptly painted portraits of Mr. Spock. Oodles of misproportioned sketches of Yoda. Smear-paint starscapes, unfunny cartoons, and other assorted drek. Plus a few pieces of good commercial art. (Note the word commercial, we'll get back to that later.) But in the main what you see displayed is garbage. Absolute rubbish in fact. Shit that one should be too embarased to display in public. Still, these morons persist on doing just that.

Here, if you don't believe me, take this for an example.

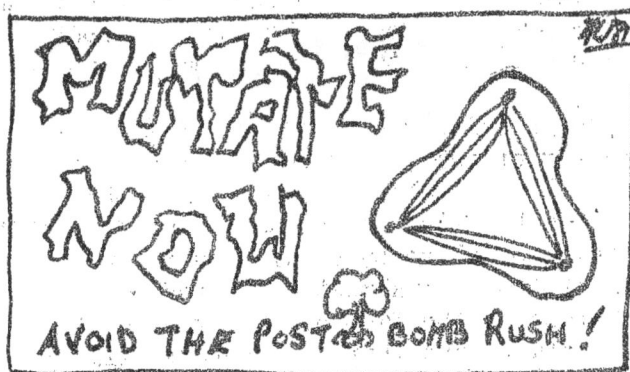

See what I mean? Now that is not art, is it? Of course, it isn't! I'll admit that it may be cute and maybe even mildly amusing, (after all, it was drawn by me), but it's not art. Nonetheless, in a fan "art" show it sold for $10.00. Do you believe that? Well it's true, anyway. Some turkey actually paid ten bucks for the above graffitti. Now let me tell you, the namebadge # (Including namebadge holder) cost me about 15¢. It took me probably a total of an hour and a half to concieve and draw that on the namebadge, incolour. So figuring at minimum wage of three bucks an hour plus a dollar bonus for creative thought the entire namebadge should have cost only, $2.65, at most three bucks. The minumum bid I placed on it was 50¢.

This is why there is so much drek in these con art shows. Because almost anyone can draw something that at least looks sort of like a person, or a dragon, or the starship Enterprize which some idiot will pay outrageous sums of money for. In other words it's a way to make a quick buck.

Above, I mentioned that fans produced good comercial art. Well, yes, some do. There are also some very good to excellant fan cartoonists, many of them better that some of the cartoonist who work for major newspapers. But no matter how well done comercial art is done, it is not ART. I can here the cries, "I know a fan who can paint as well as Kelly Freas!" Sorry but I consider Mr. Freas to be a comercial artist too. Very few of his or any other magazine artist's works would I consider to be comparable to that of a Van Gogh or Dali, or even a Tom Thompson. I'm not saying that these artists can't produce such masterpieces, not at all. In fact, some probably do. All I'm saying is the stuff you see, the stuff you glorify is not ART but either comercial art or drek.

Neil Williams

PISSING ON A PILE OF OLD AMAZINGS

...A modest column by Lester Rainsford

I'm going to ask a question, because none of you fart-assed, dog-eared, snivel-fingered, tadpoled twerps out there (who laughably enough pass as 'readers') saw fit to entertain this question in the doubtful recesses of your putative skull.

Swill is a pile of shit. You know that. I know that. Granted, the Editor doesn't, but how can you tell her from shit?

So what is someone as brilliantly perceptive as I doing writing a column for this magazine more fit for polishing the hind ends of swine than for a trendy table in Cabbagetown II? Why, in short, is my illustrious name appearing in this literary running sore?

Well, Dear Readers (who didn't ask this question, but deserve an answer to it in any case, even if I have to ram it down their thoats), fuck right off.

I'm sorry I didn't mention Guelph in the last column. Consider it ~~rectumfied~~ rectified.

In any case, life must go on, although it is somewhat disappointing to see peiople die suddenly in car crashis, thus robbing you of the opportunity to gioating 'I told you so'. This is about the only good that I can see in cigarette smoking: when the smoker lies in the cancer ward, a gaping hole where his/her/its lungs used to be, kept alive by clear plastic tubes connected to the innards, you have a lot of time and almost unlimited opportunity to smirk and breathe deeply, thus impressing the fact on the dying puffer that your lungs still are capable of oxygen uptake, and that non-smokers will live to be atleast 366 (time units your discretion), while addicted, pathologically-brained smokers, dependent in a t least three-quarters of their life processes on nicotine, will probably hack their last at about 27 years of age. Clearly, Darwinian selection rules OK.

Which brings us tho the matter of the back cover on this issue. Note please that it is Physics that rules. As we a l know (because Isaac Asimov probably said it), the ranking in the sciences is: physics, astronomy, sociology, numero-ology, te a-cup reading, biology, biochemistry, and chemistry. I invite a rebuttal from any chemist or biologist with sufficient teremity to challenge the obvious truth and correctness of this natural order. However, just to make this tough, this must be a written argument. Back to your stick-and-circle printing practice books, kiddies and IUPAC members.

Now that spring is finally here, we may well expect to see the sap rising; and, sure enough, SF cons are springing up all over the place. Or should that be sci-fi cons. They obviously give everyone a bad impression of fandom. Obnoxious horders relieving themselfves on light standards, then licking it up again (is this the ultimate in recycling?). Ugh.

Everyone could use a little social conscience, and it's time you used your teensey-weensey one. I am, of course, referring to the Save-the-Trekkie fund. If somethin isn't done very soon, these inoffensive, stupid little creatures, often sporting pells of strange designs ('Spock rools ok'), are really a menace to no one but lamp standards. When caught, the strictly should be thrown back. Only in this way may we preserve the asininity of these squint-eyed, lop-eared critters for the amusement of future generations.

Well, I'm glad you liked this month's column. You're probably only about as stupid as you look, or maybe just a wee little bit more so.

NEXT MONTH: Another wonderful column

THE AVERAGE SF. FAN

Question: What is a fan?
Answer: Someone who reads science fiction while stuffing oneself.

Q: How can you spot a fan in a crowd?
A: Just look for the zepplin wearing the Trekkie shirt.

Q: Why are fans so fat?
A: They read a lot of sf.

Q: Why don't fans move their lips when they read?
A: Their mouth is full of food.

Q: What is a fan's favourite reading material?
A: The list of ingrediants in a Vachon cake.

Q: What is a fan's second favourite reading material?
A: A potato chip wrapper.

Q: Do fans ever read science fiction?
A: Only when they run out of Vachon cakes and potato chips.

Q: Why do fans think that trashy sf. is great literature?
A: They are suffering from potato chip and Vachon cake withdrawal.

Q: What happens when you hit a fan with a horse's legbone?
A: The shin hits the fan.

Q: What happens when you hit a fan with shit?
A: You get shit all over the place.

Q: What are fandom's favourite sports?
A: The hundred twinkie dash, the 60 second pizza devour, and the hop, skip and burst.

Q: Do fans participate in any normal sports?
A: Yes, swimming.

Q: Why do fans like to swim?
A: Fat floats.

Q: Why are fans prohibbited from Atlantic Beaches?
A: The last time a fan jumped in, New York City was flooded.

Q: How can you tell a male fan from a female fan?
A: Beats us.

Q: Why are fans virgins?
A: They can't tell either.

Q: How can you tell there's a sf. convention in your area?
A: You call 967-1111 forty two times, and it's busy every time.

CONTINUED

THE AVERAGE SF. FAN (CONTINUED)

Q: How else can you tell there's a sf. con in your neighbourhood?
A The sound of dying potato chips keeps you awake all night.

Q: How can you tell there's a fan in the room?
A: You can no longer inhale.

Q: Why are fans obnoxious?
A: You're not edible.

Q: Why do fans dislike mundanes?
A: THey recognise their inferiority.

Q: Why are mundanes superior?
A: They are more intelligent.

Q: Why are fans so dumb?
A: Their brains have been smothered by the fat.

Q: Is fandom, childish, moronic, and unsuited for survival?
A: Yes.

Q: If fandom is that unfit, shouldn't it cease to survive?
A: Yes.

Q: Why does it survive?
A: Fandom is secretly supported by all major potato chip manufacturers
and pizza chains.

Q: Is there anything we can do to stop this?
A: No, unfortunately.

Q: What do you do when you see a fan?
A : Steal his Vachon cake and watch him croak from sugar deprivation.

J. S. Goobly BSc, Xenobiology

J. S. Goobly is a science student at York university. He loves to do
nasty things to his experimental animals. He is the inventer of the ratmobile,
a cart propelled by 50 rats that have been tickled under the tail. A great
lover of music, Mr. Goobly has perfected a version of the Muppetphone using
live chickens. His small business, TOAD AEROSPACE LTD (A research company to
examine the effects and design of vehicles for hardlanding toads on tarmac from a
height of seventy metres) is doing quite well, though the success rate for its
killing subjects is rather low, to say the least. J. S. Goobly is on the
Humane Society's Ten Most Wanted List and is the SPCA Animal Enemy Number One.

THEY SPACE TRIBBLES, DON'T THEY?

Let me introduce you to two terms, OSFIC and Euthanasia. OSFIC is the abreviation for the Ontario Science Fiction Club. Euthanasia is a form of murder known as mercy killing; like putting the cat to sleep. Now if any of you have a gram of brains in your skulls you should, possibly, (it's within the realm of credulity), be able to put one and one together and realise that I'm about to suggest that OSFIC be snuffed, bumped off, or otherwise put to death. If you haven't yet realised this, well that's what I am suggesting, fool!

Why am I proposing a lynch party for OSFIC? My reasons are as follows.

What is OSFIC? Supposedly it is the Ontario Science Fiction Club. Note, the key word is ONTARIO. To my knowledge, there are no OSFIC members from outside the Toronto area. In fact, there are damn few members at all. OSFIC is but a small segment of Toronto fandom. An almost dead group, that is about as active as your average comotose patient. By all rights it is dead and, really, should be dead. But no, it continues to live, slowly dying.

Whatever OSFIC, in its deteriorating state, presently is, it is not an ONTARIO science fiction club. It's not even the Toronto science fiction club. It is a blank. Nothing but a few parasites living off the empty husk of a once great organisation. There will never be another Ontario science fiction club, in the true sense of the name. Local fan groups are the rule. Local fan groups won't support a provincial group, they prefer their independance. Thus a real provincial club is not foreseeable in the near future.

But—some turkeys are presently attempting to "Revitalise" OSFIC. Why, I don't know? They like the name I guess. These pricks have no intentions of trying to create an all provincial club, or even an all Toronto club. Fine, they're not imperialists. Still, they're pompous asses since they call their little Toronto fan club, OSFIC. If these people were imperialists, I might support them, especially if they planned to even unify Toronto fandom, (something that needs to be done if we're ever going to see another good con here), although I'd have had great doubts as to their success. Imperialism isn't very fashionable these days, just ask the Soviet Union and the United States, they know. But since these morons have no such plans I can't even consider the possibility of supporting them. To be truthful, I must attack.

At present, OSFIC holds meetings and puts out a newsletter, sometimes. (If they can agree on who should put it out.) They produce no fanzines and hold no conventions. They don't even assist in the organisation of cons that other groups put on. They are—a non-group.

Therefore I call upon Toronto fandom to crush, once and for all, OSFIC. Put the name to rest. Even though it can no longer do so in dignaty, let it die. It is the only kind thing left to do. Don't let the vampires have their way! Euthanasia is often an admirable action. Or perhaps, we can get the assholes who wish to prolong the existance of OSFIC to wise up and change the name. But such an intelligent move from these people is rather too much to hope for.

Never-the-less, however it is done, OSFIC MUST DIE!!!

Neil Williams

THE SAGA OF MY FAME

NOW I AM FAMOUS... BUT WHAT GOOD IS IT

WILL FAME MAKE THIS TREE GROW?

MY FANS MIGHT

TO BE CONT'D...

THE AMERICAN WEIGH: OR, A GRAM OF BRAINS IS WORTH A POUND OF SHIT

A lot of Americans believe a lot of silly things; but, as Abraham Lincon pointed out, you can fool some of the people all of the time. And, as H.L. Menken once said, no-one went bankrupt underestimating the intelligence of the American public.

So it should not be too suprising to see that Libertarianism is quite popular down in the States. This typically American (read: brainless) philosophy is puffed up to ridiculous proportions in L.N. Smith's book The Probability Broach.

There are no doubt people who haven't read this book. There are also people who have never fallen into a sewer; both classes can consider themselves lucky.

Is this book sf? No. It is propaganda. Beside this book, Mein Kampf seems reasonable, lucid, and logical. The writing style is dismal, the characters cardboard, and the plot preposterous.

For those of you not swimming about in sewers, let me outline what this book is about.

In 1987, the U.S. is in sad shape. It is in dismal shape. We are then shown a Libertarian world where everything is WONDERFUL.

Moral. Libertarianism is WONDERFUL.

Ha ha. Hee hee. Ho ho.

For instance, in the Libertarian world (henceforth to be called OZ) science is WONDERFUL. The only trouble is that Ms. Smith knows as much about science as a Californian knows about igloos. The science in this story is not Omni-level; it is Scientology level (Sorry, Mr. Hubbard). (Well, not really sorry). Why science in a Libertarian world would progress faster is difficult to see. Note that Einstein came up with relativity, the photo-electric effect, and E=Mc while working in a patent office. A Swiss Government patent office.

Would Maxwell have thought of the electromagnetic equations earlier if he wasn't being taxed?

In fact, the science in this story is all gadgetry. For instance, 'Electrically heated streets' are mentioned. A simple, back-of-the-envelope calculatio shows that to melt the snow off the streets in a medium-sized city would require a steady power drain on the order of a gigawatt.

Perhaps they have never heard of snow shovels. Of course, these are Libertarians.

Other curiosities abound, such as fusion powered dirigibles travelling at 500km/hr-1. Perhaps Ms. Smith has never considered the etymology of 'dirigible'. It means 'not rigid'. A kilometre-long dirigible travelling at half a megametre an hour would quickly become like a patchwork quilt: one patch here, another one there, and several more patches elsewhere.

This should not be surprising. Americans are conscious, subconsciously, of their abysimal lack of culture and sophistication, and so they tend to retreat into gadgetry. ('We're not barbarians—we invented whitewall tires!!) Sure. And Attila's men decorated their horses, you know.

That's the trouble with this book: it makes no convincing case that OZ will be WONDERFUL. It simply says so. I'm sorry, but this is nonsense. I could write a book where penguins have taken over the world. I, too, could claim that it was going to be WONDERFUL.

CONTINUED

THE AMERICAN WEIGH (CONTD.)

    Oh, well, The Probability Broach was written for believers anyway. For nonbelievers, have you ever considered a penguin for a boss? Unless we accept it on blind faith, we clearly see that OZ would not work.

    There is another neat thing: the perverted emphasis on guns. It seems that guns solve every problem. Just think how wonderful it is to have your own gun. Is someone blocking the elevator door? Bang! Is someone sitting in the washroom too long? THROW A NUCLEAR HAND GRENADE OVER THE PARTITION!! BOOOM!!!

    Or art criticism: "Dali sucks." Bang! Pow!

    Yes, Americans love guns. It is, of course, their constitutional right to bear arms. A pity, though, that they have no right to carry brains; and most of them don't

    People like President Reagan are against gun control. This is why others shoot them. With guns.

    Americams, in fact, seem to think that firepower solves everthing. Just look at El Salvador. These idiot Yanks think that, by propping up a murderous, represive, anti-freedom, right-wing junta (pronounced 'yunta'), they are making the world 'safe for democracy'. Safe for the American multu-nationals, in any case.

    Isn't American democracy wonderful? Don't we all wish to preserve the American Way of Life: Jack Oswald, Charles Manson, Richard Nixon, Son of Sam, 1,096 murders in Detroit, lynchings, murders, intolerance, Monkey Trials, motherhood, and apple pie.

    Look, you stupid Americans. Why don't you take your offensive, moronic gospel shows, which actually clutter up Canadian airwaves, and stick them where a Chihuahua can't see? Why don't you take your buses with the golden eagle on front, and turn them into roosts for pidgeons? And old-time preachers? Takey your flag, your Pledge of Allegiance (no, not Lemon Pledge), and your whole damn 'grey-hat nay-ha-shun', and rotate it through n-space, so your asses wind up where your ears are (but who will notice?).

    Observe that even Kalahari bushmen have progressed beyond the stage America is at today.

    Smarten up, America, or you'll be sorry: do you see any Neanderthals about today???

P. I. Leninski, B.Sc.

To the ass--hole who calls himself editor of the most vile,disgusting
obnoxious piece of crap(in the guise of a zine) that i have ever puked
on while reading.

Dear Neil,

    Congrats on finally getting SWILL published,i know you had trouble
finding someone stupid enough to run it off for you.Not that i can blame
anyone for refusing to print it,i mean who wants to get attacked by
hordes of deranged mediafen riding rabid dragons(now getting attacked by
sheep is another story).Now on with the critizism:

    The article on mediafen left out a few things that i feel should have
been mentioned,you stated that they don't know how to read,i have to
disagree with this as i personaly meet one that could.i mean,really it
happened at a con in TO,there she was reading the latest issue of
Richie Rich,i mean that's a start,maybe in a while she won't need to
look at the pictures so closely to understand the plot,although i doubt
since she has two strikes against,being female and a media fan.

    The article that really pissed me off was the pissing on a pile of
old Amazings.i like to wear silk panties on my head and a bowler hat on
my buns and while i don't fornicate with dragons,i do fuck sheep and i'm
no depraved whacko,just ask my shrink.Also in Lester's travelogue,he
fails to mention Guelph,land of the sheep and home of all the true fen
in the world.i mean if you don't live in the big G you can't be a fan,
since youv'e never been to the infamous GSFG annual Bar-B-Q.,where we
always have at least a dozen cats roasting on the spit and bheer for
all,

    Thrash the trekkie is a fun game but i can't believe that you
would reccomend it for the whole family,no lamb of mine is allowed to
associate with any trekkie,you never know what filthy habits or diseases
the kids will come up with.i do agree though that they should be allowed
to view the bodies as an example of what can happen from watching to much
TV.The other game mentioned fun with Fritz is of course a standard
schoolyard diversion which i am sure we all played at one time or another,
it's nice to know that the old games are not forgotten.

    The last article,the Ottawa slander sheet is a misnomer in that it is
not slanderous to tell the truth.i especially agree with the statements
made about the blood-sucking dealers who always crawl out of the wood-
work at any con,they are nothing but parasites who pray on the fen in
their quest to make money at the cost of all that is holy to the true
fen.

    Keep up the good work and don't stop kicking the mediafen in the balls

                        George Oliver Dowright

Letters Of Comment

Hey, we got some locs on the first ish of SWILL. All three of them.
Comeon you mutherfuckers send us more, or else Lester will shit on your face.

Mr. Williams,
Thank you for your immaginative and creative
debunking of Sci-Fi fans. Being of the new elite minority; a Sci-Fi abstainer
I am always pleased to see the pompous idiotic trivia person exposed for what
he really is. Sci-Fi fans are merely obnoxious people who are unable to
interact socially because they are profoundly ignorant and therefore they
memorize such tidbits of wisdom as the number of the starship Enterprize and
maintain that their obscure knowledge is the justification for their arrogance.
These fan type people need something, no matter how irrelivant to mankind in
reality, to make them feel compitant with the rest of the human race from
which they are alienated. Thank you for exposing these narrow witted ninnies.

Stephano
of no fixed address

you're most welcome. we're always pleased to serve the public. by the
way, your spelling is almost as bad as ours. illiterate.   ed.

Neil,
I really liked it, but don't tell anyone I said so, or
that I've read it.

Scrotum the Unwashed

sorry scrotum. ha ha. you should have known we'd print it anyway.
tell you're brother Unbathed that we want another article. ed.

scummo,
I hear from Les that you and he are putting out a scandal
sheet. Very nice of you to send me a copy, shit head. No, seriously (hah) if
you have a copy left, I would like to see it. I also offer my services as a
world-famous writer to you. Columns written, and insults perpetrated at no charge.
If you don't mind, I would like to contribute to such a prestigious publication.
Lemme know what you want, and when you want it, and we'll see what can be done.
I have great credentials for the job. As soon as I figure out what they are, I'll
let you know. Send me a copy of the 'zine.

Tim Parker
Kuntata, (near ottawa)
ick!!!

zine and editorial requirements posted off. to any other world famous writers
out there, send us your stuff, send us your shit, we'll print it! Note: all
world famous writers must submitt their world famous writer's lisence with their
first submission. ed.

ENDNOTE: To all you turkeys, bozos, and then the select few who are smart like us,
send us articles and locs. We welcome submissions and we'll print almost anything.
SWILL costs $1.00 in canada and $1.25 in yankland. Subscription rate $9.00 per

year.

PHYSICS RULES OK!!!

and:

IUPAC SUX!

SWILL #3

April 1981

Swill

Volume One
Number 3
$1.00

™

SWILL

EDITORIAL

Isn't it great that one of the old pros of science fiction is the editor of one of the largest publishers of sf. paperbacks? Doesn't the vision of hundreds of supurbly printed, top quality sf. novels endlessly rolling off the presses come to mind? Too bad the vision is, just that, a vision.

Del Rey Books, the publishing house I'm referring to, is absolutely the worst science fiction publisher in North America. It regularly produces tonnes of ill printed, poorly written, overpriced garbage from its presses. The best thing about the majority of the novels it prints is their covers. Yes, I do concede that usually the full colour, front covers are remarkably attractive--but, so what!! Del Rey does not publish comic books (thank god). It is suposed to be printing novels and/or anthologies filled with funny little black marks which we call the printed word. This indeed it does do, but unfortunately the content quality of these printed words is so terribly inferior that one wishes that they were (and as it may sound) publishing comic books. At least we might be assured of quality in artwork, but then again, maybe that is too much to hope for from Del Rey.

The majority of Del Rey's new novels can be branded as insipid fiction, due to their profound lack of writing style, good plot, and believable characters. To draw an example, L.N. Smith's, The Probability Broach, (which was mentioned in our last issue). Not only is this a dismal novel on the grounds that it is propaganda, it is also ineptly written. Ms. Smith dates each of the chapters chonologically in relation to the sequence of events in the novel. This is not done for reasons of artistic merit but simpley because the author cannot handle juxtoposition in time. Were the dates not there, the reader would be unable to tell whether or not the action was still happening later that afternoon or two days later. The Probability Broach is a good example of the literary impotence of Del Rey's new scribblers.

Fortunately, (due to the pitiful "writing" quality of these new "authors") Del Rey publishes mostly reprints. Unfortunately, these reprints are vastly overpriced, as are most Del Rey books. Look, I terribly object to paying $2.75 for a new printing of Childhood's End. If anything, the reprints should be less expensive than the new books. The profit has already been made from the initial investment, many times over when you think of the peanuts they paid the authors when these books first appeared on the market. I would hardly object to these increases if Arthur Clarke was recieving a huge royalty for this new reprint, but (if the publishing world is as the authors say it is) I seriously doubt that his royalty payments have increased greatly, or if they've been increased at all over the past thirty odd years. And thus, all this extra money the readers have to shell out is just going to line the pockets of the profiteering bastards that rule Del Rey Books.

Fuck them! If the excess profits went back to the author (many of whom

Editor: Neil Williams
Columnist: Lester Rainsford
Book Reviewer: Illy Litrate

Contributers: G.O. Dowright,
          Count Eric von Schicklegruber III
          Alicia Longspear

Art: Kevin Davies, Stephano, EDART

SWILL April 1981   © 1981 Vile Fen Press

SWILL Volume 1, Number 3. 46 Radford Ave, Toronto, Ontario, CANADA.
     $1.00 Canadian, $1.25 American.   Subscriptions: $8.00 per year.

that do need the money) or reinvested toward the purchase of good fiction and quality printing, I wouldn't bitch. But it isn't! Del Rey just mouths the same reason as the rest of them in the industry; increased paper costs. Uh, excuse me, but the cost of paper has not risen that much, boardroom boys. If it had risen as high as you would make it appear, I wouldn't be able to afford to print this little magazine. So cut the bullshit, Del Rey!!!

The last comment I have to make is on the planned obsolecence in Del Rey paperbacks. I am talking about the new-fangled self-destruct book. The majority of the print run of J.P. Hogan's new book, Thrice Upon A Time (a Del Rey book that ain't that bad) is a perfect example of this brilliant idea. To read this novel one must have it opened at no greater than a 30° angle, which makes the book very difficult and not very enjoyable to read. Why an angle no greater than thirty degrees? Because, if you open it to any greater angle the annoying sound of, "crack", is heard as yet another page falls out from the non-existant binding. Obviously, this has been done to curb the resale of Del Rey novels to used book stores, the book can only be read once. Another neat idea that Del Rey has come up with is miscollating. In my copy of Thrice Upon A Time, when you get to page fifty one discovers that the next twenty pages are not 51-70 but 121-140. Wonderful, except between the pages 120 and 141 are also pages 121-140. Perhaps Del Rey believes that these twenty pages are so good, they deserve to be read twice.

Is there a solution to this problem? You bet. Del Rey isn't going to listen to letters, pleas, or petitions. They don't give a damn about their readers; they've already shown that to us. What must be done is to hit these money-grubbing propertarians where it counts, in their financial statement. Then, maybe they'll listen to us. Just stop buying Del Rey books, unless they happen to be on the used book shelf, where the price is, to some degree, more reasonable. So, kick the assholes where it really hurts. In that way we just might see a pleasant change in their publishing policy. If not, maybe they'll go belly up, floating in their own literary excrement and bloated by their ill-gotten gains till they sink forever into their stagnant pool of shit.

BOYCOTT DEL REY BOOKS!!!!! What have YOU got to lose?

Neil Williams

FUN AND GAMES FOR ENLIGHTENED COUPLES
-- OR, WHAT TO DO UNTIL YOUR PARTNER COMES   --Alicia Longspear

Contrary to the chauvinistic ideology of SWILL, there are some intelligent readers of sci-fi, and it is to them that I direct this article. For they are sci-fi readers (and, what is worse, SWILL readers), so clearly 'intelligent' does not mean 'aware'. I trust my modest efforts to instill awareness will be successful.

It comes as no surprise to anyone that sci-fi is a masculine-sexist, repressive organisation, determined to subjugate the naturally-superior female. Reading any of the so-called 'classics' from the Thirties through to the early Seventies ought to illustrate clearly the subtle but all-prevasive characterisation of females as bedroom decorations inferior to the lowly shag throw-carpet, which at least is washable, develops no headaches, has no aspirations to occupy its rightful place at the apex of civilisation, and in any case comes with a ten-year 'no-wear-thru' (sic) guarantee. Recently, however, it has become trendy to 'analyse' sci-fi's sexual content. This pretence at an 'objective' analysis is, again, simply a thinly-disguised plot to demonstrate the 'superiority' of the male. What is more symbolic of sci-fi than a rocketship? And what is a rocketship, according to this echt-bourgeois Freudian analysis that a penis? (A 'penis', for those of you lucky enough to be unacquainted with this disgusting object, is the long,fleshy urinary tube of the male. Occasionally, they stiffen it--possibly with coat-hanger wire--and try, for their own ineluctable purposes, to poke it into you and fill you up with a nasty smelly sticky substance. Since your lover will afterwards complain that she has to keep washing her finger off, this is best avoided.)

What should the intelligent sci-fi fan do about all this? Well, first she should buy an assortment of vibrators. Then, if she's enthusiastic, she should buy a Vice-Grip with good, sharp, shiny, carbon-hardened steel teeth. The vibrators have their customary use. So do the Vice-Grips.

Of course, some misguidedly idealistic people will attempt to convert their male 'brethern' to the truthful way through impassioned argument. This is roughly akin to trying to persuade a rock to fly. The only way a rock will fly is if you throw it, and the only way to convince males of your superiority is to hoof 'em in the danglies and watch 'em retch. Not only is this swifter, it is much more fun.

And, remembering your AS/ENG 101.6, dangling participles whould always be excised.

The obvious best place to strike back at the arrogant puerile male sci-fi 'fan' (not reader; they are generally too fat to see beyond their own pimples) is at a sci-fi 'convention'. Now in general these 'cons' are merely an excuse for these deprived and depraved males to stage a wild orgy, complete with gang-rapes of socks, fur mittens, rolled-up programmes, cigarette burns in upholstery, and small elbow macaroni. They are also the times that males consume incredible quantities of liquour to drown their sorrow at being born male and inferior. Now I realise that some people will claim that 'you can't choose whether you're born a person or male', but this argument is crap. The clever ones, realising which sex is superior, clearly arranged to be female. The dummies, not being cognisant of the choices available to them, wound up males. And then they wonder why being female is better. Well, once a dummy, always a dummy.

Back to the convention (no, really you don't have to go). It is always amusing to insert a christmass-tree lamp socket in their fur gloves. This is even more fun at European conventions, where standard voltage is 240V rather that the standard North American 120v. Another way, if you have a good healthy female body, is to go to the costume ball in a scanty costume. All the males, of course, will lustfully ogle the divinely-mandated, geometrically-perfect lines of your body. At this point, you simply set off your large-size magnesium flare, and blow the little lechers' eyeballs to ratshit. (Note: remember to tell all the femalse in the hall to look the other way.)

However, the best thing to do is to avoid sci-fi and its swinish inhabitants entirely. Left to themselves, these obese males will die out and bother us no more, although it is entirely within the realm of possibility that some of them will grow so fat that, through mitosis, they will split apart into two obese sci-fi fans. However, eventually, this strain will grow so fat that they will burst, and trouble no one any longer, except perhaps the janitors.

FEMFEN

the lurking danger

I have been greatly disturbed in recent years by the emergence of
the weaker sex into fandom.I am not arguing the fact that some are needed
to service the PRO's and the BNF's(who only get fucked at cons)but when
they start having panels about women in S.F. they're going to far.It's
bad enough that they can actually vote for the HUGOS but now they want
panels.If any of them could master the fine art of zine publishing they
would probably have their own feminist zine(I know it sounds crazy but
there is always some turncoat male that will help them)I mean how can
they get a zine out when they are bitchy for four or five days of every
month.

The insidious methods employed by these so called feminists(more like
female supramundanists) knows no bounds,why,at the last con I was refused
sex by one of these misguided women because ,as she said ,I was a male
chauvinist pig.Of course I ignored her protests and '' porked'' her any-
way(as is my male right),though I must admit it wasn't the best ''piece''
I've had,what with all the struggling until I got my cock in and she
began to enjoy it.That's the last time though that I will ever give her
the pleasure of my company,no matter how much she begs me,let her get
friendly with a dildo from now on or with the tongue of one of her feminist
friends.

This lunacy is even creeping into the costume balls where some women
are actually wearing outfits that conceal their breasts.Whats the sense of
them having tits if they aren't going to use them in the manner GHOD
intended them for,giving pleasure to men.Next thing you know they will have
women running Worldcon masquerades barring outright nudity.Once this occurs
they will start refusing to liberate swiming pools at cons or participating
in Jacuzzi parties.Can you imagine a Worldcon without a lime-green-dream?
Just the thought of it makes me shiver in rage.

Now you are asking what we as ''real men'' and true fen can do about
this lurking danger?Well for a start refuse to honour these so-called women
with the pleasures of your cock,I mean we don't really need women to get
off,if we did GHOD wouldn't have given us hands or allowed fur gloves to
be manufactured.Also I hate to admit it but some of you have neglected to
beat your women reguarly,get back into the weekly habit and show them you
really care.They all love the feel of the lash (just ask Tarl Cabot) and if
they get it at home they won't need to stray and fall into the clutches of
the feminists.Now come on men lets work together and get our women back
where they belong,in the kitchen and the bedroom of our homes and eradicate
this dangerous feminist movement before it spreads to far.

G.O.Dowright

PISSING ON A PILE OF OLD AMAZINGS

....a modest column by Lester Rainsford

Hello out there, people....and science fiction fans. You know, one of the more interesting theories espoused by the toads (Damon Knight's words, not mine) who hop through the sci-fi world is that sci-fi is a literature (their word, not mine) of ideas. This, they claim, is what makes sci-fi superior to that dull mainstream stuff which is all about people and trolley-bus routes and the rest of that crap.

You see, if sci-fi is a literature of ideas , it is obviously the stuff of intellectuals and thinking toads people. And them wot think can't be all that bad, can they? In fact, these are them wot are not surprised by new developments (atom bombs, space travel, lemon-flavoured potato chips), but are instead in the vanguard of truth, progress, and the American Way.

Well this is all fine and dandy, except for one slight flaw of reasoning, which however is significant enought a crack in the foundations of this arrogantly elitist and hoity-toity notion to cause the entire edifice to crack down the maiddle and, like Poe's House of Usher, fall quietly into the tarn, while a balefully full moon, rising, looks on.

And what is this fatal flaw, you ask? Not surprising—that you ask, I mean—because if you were smart enough to notice the flaw you would be writing this column, not me. And note, please, that I only work secure jobs.

All right, I suppose I've kept you in suspense long enough. So best I tell you.

As it happens, the idea that it is a world of ideas is about the only idea that the sci-fi has, and it's a pretty poor notion at that. What justification is there for this idealistic view of sci-fi? Actually, none at all.

Well of course we would eliminate the thud-and-blunder fantasy stuff right away (I do not think anyone would argue with that), as well as the soft-core stuff of Norton, Lee, Vance, Laumer, Zelazny, and so forth. I don't feel that it is even worth discussing the idea content of their books, which in any case run to cutsey worlds, improbable adventures, and stalwart heroes. Or nonstalwart heroes, which is even more boring.

What, then, of those writers who supposedly put a great deal of idea content into their works? Any list of these authors would have to include most of sci-fi's heavyweights: Asimov, Heinlein, Clarke, Anderson, Van Vogt, Dickson, and so on, as well as the so-called 'hard-core' writers (whose work might well be better described by the term 'apple core'—what's left after all the good stuff has been eaten), such as Clement, Niven, Sheffield, Hogan, and Howard.

But where are the ideas in this supposedly illustrious list of sci-fi 'greats'? Well, Van Vogt and Heinlein (as well as authors—I hesitate to call them people—such as L Neil Smith) are peddlers of purile right-wing reactionary Republicanism and the notion of the big storng male (but of course) hero. Where are their ideas? Have they anticipated the more enlightened things—ERA, ecological consciousness, the individual's duty to society, rather that vice-versa—that seem to be harpening now? Ha! Rather, they are strikingly backward proponents of the way things were thirty or forty years ago, where them that had could perfectly well kick in the balls (and tits) of them that didn't, in order to retain their 'superiority'

What striking new ideas are contained in Asimov? The Foundation trilogy, his most famous work, is based wholesale on Gibbon's Decline and Fall of the Roman Empire, which itself is not exactly an original work of fiction. Furthermore, it happens that Gibbon puts across all the ideas Asimov talks about, only more effectively. But sci-fi fans, being idea people, do not care to know about history. But put this empire in space and—zowie!! Profound messages! Even more profound than Star Wars (well, occasionally, anyway).

I still have a lot to say, but I see that I'm running out of sapce. So, I think I'll continue these ruminations next month—unless no one appears to be interested, in which case I will discuss favourite TTC routes that I have known.

PS: If you don't believe a word I'm saying, go ride the Bay 6 trolley right into Lake Ontario. Then come and discuss it with me.

Twinkle, Twinkle, Little Laser

Count Eric von Schicklegruber III

Pity the poor science fiction fan. Whenever he enters a store to buy a book, he heads for his favorite section, usually conspicuously labelled "Science Fiction/Fantasy". Why, oh WHY must they add that last bit? Sf is not Fantasy (thank Charlton Heston), nor is Fantasy sf. A look at most store's selection will reveal a few sf book, turned so only their spines are visible, sandwiched between a couple of fantasy books with garish covers. Inevitably, one has a naked (or semi-naked) women (always big-breasted) posing in some unseemly pose with a dragon. (See Swill Vol 1 No 1) The other has a man that could be Mr Universe clenching a gleaming sword in his hand, muscles bulging, loin cloth bulging (with Kleenex). And the pattern is repeated over, and over, and over....

And the fantasy books are all the same. Sure, the characters name changes, and the planet's name changes, and the monster's name and number of tentacles changes, but other than that, it has a marked similarity to every other book ever written in the fantasy field. Well, friends, I have managed to uncover the reason...after years of diligent research, it can now be told. Deep in the vaults of a publisher's warehouse, sits a microcomputer. Back in the early days, a fantasy story was copied into its memory banks from a pulp magazine. A program was written that will randomly choose letters to make up names, places, and dates, and the computer substitutes the variables into the text. Next, an artist draws a monster and girl, and voila, a brand new, amazing, totally new fantasy book. Complete with magic spells, and flying carpets. Yipee shit. I read SF not fantasy. Please, booksellers, remove the "/Fantasy" from my section and place it where it belongs. "Humour/Fantasy" sounds good.

Alas but the world still isn't safe from Trekkies. A few weeks ago I turned on my VDTV and saw a phone-in program dealing with "The Star Trek Phenomenon". That by itself is okay, I like a good laugh every now and then. And the wonderful art by these fans was miraculous in its badness. But what bugs the crap out of me most is the reasons given for watching Trek. The "Trekkers" as opposed to "trekkies" watch 'Trek because of the underlying messages of brotherhood, human error, non-rascist, detante, world unity, etc ad nauseum. To which I reply BULLSHITTIES! They watch it cause they like to see Spock say something witty to Kirk. They like Spock's pointed little ears, and most of all, they like...Tribbles. Girls love Spock. Boys love Tribbles. The Universe is whole again. Please, you asshole Trekkers admit it. You watch Trek cause its fun! (But then, so's peeling the skin of aardvarks.)

I met a publisher of sf books last month. He was typical of the sf publishers in this cruddy little world. He don't know one pissing thing about sf. He thinks Pohl Anderson has to do with the John Anderson election campaign. He thought Tanith Lee was something like Tennis Elbow. Why must we face up to these cretins, who don't know good sf from a hole in the ground. Tell your MP's: we want good sf. After all, the political process in Canada is a good example of sf.

BUK RIVOOS

By Illy Litrate

347 Things to do With A Rubber Stopper by F.E.Tish, Afun Pubs, 26.98
      Although at first glance this book may appear overpriced at
almost twenty-seven dollars, it is well worth every penny. The
vast number of innovative ideas included change one's opinion of
the rubber stopper from something that has only one purpose, to
a miracle of engineering that can solve all the world's problems.
In the first two chapters, Tish explains the intricate process by
which a rubber stopper is made; the care necessary to ensure complete rubber polymerization, through to the fine shaping of the
finished product. In Chapter 3, Tish examines the history of
this invention, from the conception by Da Vinci (during a diarrhea
attack) to Gen. Eisenhowers plan to place them in every Panzer
tank's armament at night. From there, Tish lists the 347 different
purposes a clever stopper-user can put his stopper to use as (?).
For example, did it ever occur to anyone that a hole drilled
into a stopper allows its use as an erection aid?, or that drilling
only half way through the stopper gives a condom?, or the fact
that fifty stoppers glued one on top of the other makes an excellent
dildoe? This amazing tome is a necessity for every true book
lover. Get it now.

Gourmet Cooking With Tribble Stew by Trudge & Swill, Tripleday, 0.75
      Aside from the obvious bargain at 75¢, this book is the
bachelor's salvation. From a lowly can of Tribble Stew, many
gastronomical delights such as Duck à la Tribble, Chateaux Tribble,
and the staple Tribble à la King can be concocted. This book
shows you in intense color, the steps to follow for hundreds of
these delights. Buy the book now...great for fantrips!

The Empire Gets Kicked In The Balls by G Locust, Fandom House, 7.95
      Second in the series of one, this sequel to the bestseller
(five editions abroad) follws Hand Job and his Woolie through
the galaxies in their attempt to find the true meaning of it
all. Their stopovers on the scummy planets of the universe are
loving detailed, down to every lowlife and galactic reject.
Highlights are the fart scene, and the trip through the Hemmorhoid
field. As always, the Farce is with them. The Galactic Emperor
makes an appearance with a hologram of Mac Tse Tung in the
climactic climax. Does Hand find the truth? I won't give away
the ending. They don't.

Next Month:
      Watch for reviews by this intrepid (insipid) reviewer of
RingWorm Engineers, The Hitchhiker's Guide to Brambles, and
the latest bestseller, Expanded Balloon, plus more.

and now, some LOCs

I was laying in a field of tall grass the other day getting spaced out on some really good Columbian marjuanna when suddenly I experianced a revelation. Like; wow man! What is this science fiction stuff anyways?

Does science fiction advocate world peace? Does science fiction advocate free love? Does science fiction stand for the legalization of cocaine? Shit no!!!

Hey man; I know that science fiction is mind expanding and mind altering but, is this really where it is at? Just meditateing on marajuanna is the same thing. If i get a good high then not only do I dream about outer space but good acid takes me there. There is a difference man. I can't get into the escapeism of reading science fiction man. I need to really go there, into outer space, man, by taking really good drugs.

Wow what a trip man. My eyes are burning. Fuck that beatiful "Klingon". Wow my mind is so open man. My hair is electric. Wow I dig the rock and roll music on the F.M. soundwaves of marjuanna.

Fuck this science fiction man. It is a downer. It doesn't get me off man. I just stare at science fiction man. Science fiction is only good to "veg out" looking at when I get the mundies.

What useful purpose is science fiction then? What good are these countless pages of mind altering bunk and women flying around in their underwear? What good is Swill? Well; when I run out of rolling papers your science fiction magazine is the first thing I look for to rip into 1" by 2" strips. Science fiction rolling papers burn the marjuanna slow and I've never had a bad trip!

Ruby Beroach (last of the hippies)
York University

Hey, man. Like your letter was real wild. I could really, like—get into it. Wow. But I hope this doesn't, like, crush your concept of self but—SWILL makes shitty rolling papers! The paper's too thick, moran. You'd have to already be ripped to even try it. 4 by 7 centimetre strips from shredded Isaac Asimov's SF. 'Zine are much, much better. I suggest you try those in the future. ed.

Dear Niel

Ever since I begging to red your wonderfully megazine I've have now got more brain and smarter. But I gain 50 pound.

Signed
A Science Fiction fan.

Glad to hear of your progress. Amazed that you were able to read SWILL. Perhaps you should try reading this issue while riding an exercise bicycle rather than while consuming 47 Big Macs. ed.

AND MORE LOC'S

Dear Neil:
            (Good joke, that)
        Thank you for the tea bag. It was delicious. The wrapper left
a lot to be desired. Actually it was ripped. Better tape up the
next one.
        I look forward to seeing Swill No 2. (Now I suppose you wanna
know how I liked Swill No 1) Well I'll tell ya. I werent bad.
Certainly provided a giggle or tow. Keep it up, if the bank book
allows it.
        As for Swill 1, *Leskr's* colum werent bad. Typical *Les*.
liked the bit about Van Gogh. He must have been up all night
thinking it up. hest was not so hot. Liked Fun and Games.
May have to write column on holeplayinggames at some point in the
distant future. Mapleconn slandershit I saw before. LOC was
a cackle too. Not bad. Liked the cover. Must have hired an expensive
artist, eh? Needs to be longer, though. Enter my subscription
now. Three copies an issue for the next two lifetimes. Send
bill to OSFIC.

                                                T. Parker
                                        Still in Kuntata (near Hull)

        Glad you liked the teabag and SWILL 1. I liked your lollipop and articles,
    the cyanide flavouring on the lollipop was wonderful. I ate the articles and
    I'm going to print the lolipop. Okay? Your subscription order has been processed.
    OSFIC is not pleased with the bill for $661.50. They refuse to pay it, but I
    have a feeling Jimmy and Greek collection agency (Mafia Registration #47651) will
    change their minds. PLEASE send your world famous writer's licence with your next
    submission, scumo! ed.

    Editor sirs, who liking to eat shit anyway:

    I recently having misfortune of having wonderful article published in assholed
magazine yours. This experience even more dismal that exiled in Siberia eating flies
so to demonstrate ineluctable superiority of sozailism over capitalist running dogs.
First I have my name mangled to P. I. Lenininsky recalling maybe arch-capitalist composer
Pietr Illich Tchaikovsky, perpetrating of Tsarist 1812 Overture. I being Vladimir Ilych
Lenininsky. Cattle turds. Also, editors seen fit to rewrite Einstein. E=Mc forsooth
as Pink Panther saing so often. Really is $E=mc^2$. Pig snouts. Also seeing error
500km/hr-1. Clearly to have been 500 km hr^{-1}. Goat lips.
    Still, is to appreciate fan article. But is what Vachon cake?
    Also knowing in Russia My Fame approved way of making trees grow on tundra.
    Thus to eat shit capitalist swine.

                            Vladimir Ilich Lenininsky
                            Upper Yakutsk
                            Just left of the red Risk pieces holding Kamchatka

            Just be thankful that the pieces are red!   ed.

ENDNOTE

One of my contributers and a fellow editor both asked me the same question a few weeks back, "Is SWILL nasty and obnoxious just for the sake of being nasty and obnoxious?" To be truthful, the only answer I could give them at that time was, "I don't know." Well after some thought, not much but some, I can now answer that question with, "Not really." Very ambiguous, eh? Well, I'll clear that up in a moment, maybe.

That same contributer asked me another question, (this all ties together, you see.), "What is the purpose of SWILL?" The answer to that question is thus— SWILL's purpose is to criticise both science fiction and science fiction fandom. As mentioned in the editorial of the first issue (back issues are available) there is a lot of things going on in these two areas that we don't like, and therefore these things shall be criticised. This criticism takes the form of nasty and obnoxious articles attacking in the vilest manner possible the fault or problem. But, nonetheless, these articles have a point (Well, at least most of them do.) Of course, some people may find this form of criticism offensive. Tough shit! Note that the title of this 'Zine is SWILL not the Oxford Journal of Science Fiction Commentry! So don't expect any high-brow literary commentary here.

Of course, some of our articles are meant as humour. We like to have fun too. The fat fan article and the guest editorial in last issue were such examples of this. So were the fun and games page and the maplecon 3 slandersheet of the first issue. If any of our readers found these offensive, tough shit, again!

A note on the maplecon 3 slandersheet. This page was written before the con and distributed there as well, as a joke. The fact that what was written on the flyer turned out to become reality is not our fault at all.

Thus, this should give anyone who gives a damn, an idea of what we're up to. If you like it, fine. If you don't, once again, TOUGH SHIT!!!

CONTEST

On the back cover of this issue there is a picture. There are some things wrong with this picture. If you can figure out what these things are drop us a line telling us so. If you can spot all the problems, you'll receive a prize. Good enough?

NOW, YOU TOO, CAN BECOME A SWILLO!!
(You don't have to sit on the park bench any longer.)

Yes reader, here is your once in a lifetime opportunity to become a full member of the club that everyone is talking about (behind your back). You too can now become a full-fledged member of the SWILLO ORGANISATION and be entitled to all membership rights, privillages, discounts, freebees, awards (and penalties). What are you waiting for! Just tear off this handy application form and send it along with one dollar to this prestigious magazine's mailing address.

Name: _____   Occupation: _____

ADDRESS: _____   Signature: _____

Age: If under 21: _____

SO THAT YOU DON'T FORGET, MAIL THIS COUPON BY MIDNIGHT TONIGHT!!!

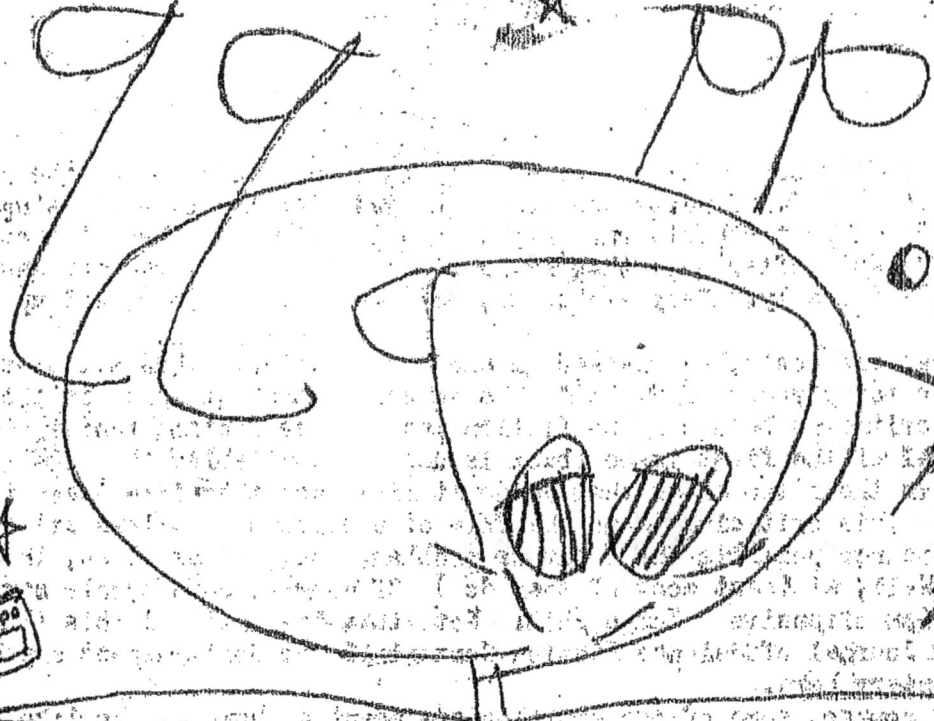

The ELVIS DIETS in SPACE!!

You recieved this wonder of literary excellance because:

☐ We think you'll like it.
☐ We think you'll hate it. (tough shit!)
☐ You are a depraved wacko.
☐ You contributed to it. (Use the toilet next time, please.)
☐ You bought it. (Dummy)
☐ You're a subscriber! (You're even dumber!)
☐ You are wonderful, maybe.
      (Note: only we are WONDERFUL!!!)

SWILL RULES O.K.!!!

SWILL #4

May 1981

VOL.1 NO 4 $1

1 SWILL

12 GRAMS

EDITORIAL

The oldtimers of science fiction, readers and writers alike, must be disillusioned with the world in its present state. The dreams that they once visualised in their youth have gone awray. Some have come true, but many others have been discarded as society regressed.

What were these dreams, ideals? Oh, nothing much, really. Just the abolishion of war, equal redistribution of resouces, world government, and the conquest of space. Those are just the major ideals, of which, only one has come to pass.

The conquest of space, or in Forties terms, landing man on the Moon has been accomplished. Many forties visionaries predicted that we'd just be able to do it now, not twelve years earlier , as was the case. Of course, how and why it was done is not the way they believed things would happen. They believed that it would be a co-opperative effort from an international space agency, that we'd have a permanent manned space station in orbit before we attempted to launch a Moon shot. Unfortunately, that is not what happened. One nation, for the sole sake of national prestige (which it sorely needed due to the unpopular war it was then fighting) landed man on the Moon. No space platform, no international effort, just a big, expendable, Earth-launched rocket and one nation lusting for fame. Of course, we did land on the Moon. The oldtimers should be amazed that at least we managed to do that.

As for their other dreams? There's a war going on every day somewhere in the world. Three quarters of the planet's population starves in poverty while the other one quarter lives in luxury. Mankind is disunited and we'll probably see global destruction rather than a world government in the forseeable future. In other words, with the exception of medical and technological advancements, we're more screwed up than we were in the forties. Science and Technology have lept forward, but society, having taken only one small step (depending on the country, Sweden has taken a big step, the U.S. has hardly taken a step at all) forward is now rallying forces to make a great leap backward.

If an attempt was made to impliment these lost ideals we could, quite possibly, create a better world. But unfortunately, these ideals lack in popularity. They are, SOCIALISTIC, or maybe even COMMUNISTIC, which is very unpopular with the rulers of this part of the world since it disagrees with the American perspective on reality.

Note; any Americans, there is a difference between the terms socialism and communism, even though you may not think so. Communism does not exist in this world, except on the small scale in Isrealli Kibutz's. Socialism is, in one form or another, the form of government that the Soviet Union, China, and their respective allies live under. It is also the form of government that most of your allies in the industrialised world live under, to a lesser and greater degree depending on the nation. The main difference between the "good guys" and "bad guys" is that the "bad guys" are totalitarian and the "Good guys" are democratic. Still, socialistic ideals are not welcome south of the border, and most Americans are shocked to learn that most of their allies are "pinkos".

CONTD. ———➤

Editor: Neil Williams

Columnists: Lester Rainsford
Illy Litrate

Contributers: Andrew Hoyt,Stephano, J.R.,
Count Eric von Schicklrgruber 3

Art: Stephano, Neil Williams
Cover by: Loblaws Ad Department

bb

SWILL: Volume 1 Number 4

Printed by: Pete Roberts
46 Radford avenue, Toronto Ontario CANADA

© MAY / 1981

EDITORIAL CONTD.

Why these ideals are not acceptable, I don't know. They appear to make more sense. Isn't it more practical for people to work together rather than killing each other or trying to grind the other guy into the mud? Doesn't it make more sense that one doesn't make friends by starving them to death and if one does so, he loses friends rapidly. That it is more efficiant to distribute resouces equally and to have such distribution ecconomically managed? Let's face it, the industrialised world wastes one hell of a lot of resources, needlessly in the pursuit of profit, that the third world would be glad to have, and need. Just think of how many eggs the Egg Marketing Board chucked out last year because they couldn't make a profit on them. Canada can, and often does, produce more grain than it can sell. What happens to this excess grain? It rots in the silos or in storage. Why not give the unsold grain away? You could save the storage fee and maybe even get a tax deduction for the loss. As for transportation, I'm sure many third world nations and relief organisationd would gladly pay the cost of transporting FREE grain.

The unification of man and the abolishment of poverty are two rather sane ideals. I'm not saying that the accomplishment of these goals will be easy. They'll be damn difficult to accomplish. But the problems are not going to solve themselves.

Americans seem to believe that as they get richer, everyone else gets richer. Wrong! In fact, the present American ecconomic slump proves this. When one country gets richer it is usually at the expense of another country's economy. Right now, Japan is getting richer at the expense of the U.S. and the rest of the industrialised world. Still the above belief is mouth by the American's neo-conservatives and libertarians. These people don't believe in the rich getting richer and the poor getting poorer (which studies have proved to be the case) but that, as the rich get richer the poor get richer. Bullshit! Isn't about time that you boys scrapped your little keynsian diagrams, which have long ago been proven not to be applicable on the large scale with any measure of success or accuracy?

If the industrialised world continues on its present course it shall, if the world survives, create a new caste system. Actually this caste system is already here but if no changes are made, the rift will widen and this division shall become more apparent. The two castes being the rich, industrial north which will economically rule the poor, agrairian south. Should we continue on this course, off planet, then the rift will become even more pronounced. True, we may force, through this manner, an industrial revolution in many third world countries, but what good is that really. They'll be entering their first industrial revolution as we are entering our third. They won't be catching up, they'll either be falling further behind or just keeping pade, at the bottom.

If we want to give a fair shake to the majority of the people on this planet, we should attempt to impliment some of those ideals found in forties science fiction. The problem of the third world won't go away. It'll stay with us, and the longer it doe the larger and more dangerous that problem will become.

Neil Williams

PISSING ON A PILE OF OLD AMAZINGS

....A modest column by Lester Rainsford

Since last month's column on the Burning Issues of the Day raised about as much reaction as a planted porcupine, I simply will have to follow through the threat of last month, and discuss TTC routes I have known. Now some of you, never having left the hick towns like Wildfield, Guelph, and New York City may not know what 'TTC' stands for. Well, to enlighten you horribly provincial toadstools, need I only say that it signifies the Toronto Transit Commission?

The Wonderful TTC runs its glorious buses, streetcars, subways, and trolley buses all over Metro Toronto. Although it is not all that wonderful when it, in the middle of January, forces one to redevelop the Principle of the Bus, viz: A bus always leaves the stop fifteen seconds before you arrive at it. And the First Corollary to the Principle of the Bus: If you arrive at the stop early enough so that you cannot possibly miss the bus, the bus will be half-an-hour late.

However, there are nice, interesting, and occasionally frustrating, TTC routes, and some of these I will now discuss.

The most interesting streetcar route is obviously the 507. In olden days, before the TTC converted all streetcar route names to numbers, because the marquees of the new UTDC streetcars were not wide enough to accomodate actual real names, the 507 was the Long Branch route. Since one of the terminuses (termini?) is also Long Branch, one was treated to the sight of streetcars rolling along Lakeshore Boulevard, destination signs proudly proclaiming Long Branch Long Branch. Now, of course, they say 507 Long Branch, which is hardly so interesting. When touring this route, be sure to wait for one of the old PCC cars, as the esthetic experience is immeasurably heightened as compared to the hatty, nasty UTDC humboxes. The Long Branch route affords one a great selection of Forties and early Fifties architecture—Lakeshore Boulevard, through Long Branch, New Toronto, and Mimico, has been steadily decaying since at least 1956—and the sight is much improved by the simple act of viewing it from a Forties or early Fifties streetcar. Unfortunately, the big snag with the Long Branch route is that it neither originates nor terminates anywhere remotely useful. Neither Long Branch (almost Mississauga, for God's sake!), nor the scummy Humber Loop, are my ideas of class acts. Still, from the Humber one can catch a 501 (nee Queen car) downtown, where civilisation lives. (This is downtown Toronto, not downtown Mississauge. Perhaps downtown Mississauge does not exist. But then, perhaps it does; if so, one of the most arguments for euthanasia has been tragically overlooked.)

Suppose one wants to take a trolley bus, (ugh) diesel bus, or subway? Where then does one turn one's attention?

This is an exceedingly complex topic, and I will return to it next column--unless I get no reaction, in which case I will have no recourse but to return to Burning Issues of the day. Perhaps they will extend to the problem of the TTC intending to change its 60-year-old colour schemes. Certainly no one can deny that this may well have a significantly destabilising effect on Western Civilisation. Whether anything good can come of this will have to be examined closely.

NEXT MONTH--Can the world survive the $29.75 Metropass?

The Shape Of Things That Are

I seldom get depressed, but a recent visit to the local bookmonger managed to do it. In the far back corner, under a small hanging sign that read "Science Fiction/Fantasy" it happened.

After elbowing my way through a maze of stalls, and pushing past adults hiding a copy of Penthouse in Better Homes and Gardens, I reached the area. "Aha!" I thunkt to myself. "At last, a place to purchase my favorite reading materials!" You see, from a distance, I could detect three set of shelves ("browsers" in the industry) devoted to my subject. Upon reaching this mecca I began my usual routine, beginning at the left, top shelf, scanning titles shelf by shelf.

As this continued, I began to get depressed. By the end of the last shelf, I was in dispair. This bookseller to the nation considered "Science Fiction/Fantasy" to consist of the large size 'illustrated' editions of Star Wars, Empire, and various other mass market goodies, a complete set of Tolkein, the Foundation series, and a couple of Heinlein's. Need I say which ones? The only exception was a Fall '79 edition of Destinies, tucked behind a 1.75 edition of Childhood's End. Somewhat in a daze, I cornered one of the employees (itself no mean trick) and managed to get her at least in a position that she could hear me. (By the way, why do bookstores always seem to hire overwieght, pimply, illiterate, prepubescent girls?)

"Is this all the sf you have?" I asked her. I admit here that I had already made my first grave error. Assuming these employees have an intelligence is not only silly, but very fatalistic.

"SF?" she asked, a stunned look on her face. (They train for weeks to perfect that look.)

"Sf: science fiction." I explained.

She brightened. "Oh, I see. Star Wars, you mean."

"Well, yes," I thought it wise not to provoke her any further. "Is this all you have?"

Ah, now, gentle reader, you seem what being depressed does to me. Normally I would have been more careful. As it was, I managed to land exactly in the trap she had worked so carefully to get me in. She waved a grubby paw at the section, and asked "You mean there's more than this?"

Now I'm not a masochist. I left.

However, a survey of all the local bookstores seem to bear out the sad truth. The stores only stock the guaranteed sellers. As a friend of mine (who works in the book industry) told me, why should a bookseller stock the esoteric titles by authors such as Haldeman, Varley, Niven, Pohl, etc, who are not sure to sell out in a month. Star Wars, they point out, sold five million copies. Can Spider Robinson match that? Besides, they inevitabley end up, there is no demand for the books. No one asks them to order the varied titles, therefore, the sf fandom remains a small, insignificant clique.

Maybe someone should tell them the truth.

Andrew Hoyt

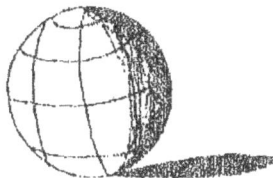

Nazi War Criminal Is German Whore Criminal

"I never did love Eva von Braun",claimed Dolly Parton look alike Suzie Weaver. Miss Weaver, now 64,claims that her opening of the Adolf Hitler Fast Food Franchise is purely "a coincedence.It is the plan of Miss Weaver to have the planned opening of a Kosher delicatesion approved by her Rabi, Herman Schultz. Schultz was a friend of Dr.Weisen in Barrie Ontario and a renouned organizor of World-Con-1945. Heil.

News To The World...Flash:Flasher

Last Sunday in London England a man, Richard Rainsworth, was arrested for flashing his tatoo to a 83 year old woman. The tatoo is reputed to have been etched across the man's genitals from the upper pubic hair region to behind his anus. The tatoo entailed the word "SCIENCE"and was followed by the letters "FI T O ". The 83 year old woman(name withheld) is reported to have said,"How quaint, I looked at least 15minutes for CI.",

MOTOWN FEMINISTS PROTEST TESTICLES

Reports from Detroit Michigan recently confirmed that the Woman"s Liberation Group "THE SISTERS NATIONAL-GROUP AGAINST PUBES" has expressed it's outrage with the publication and distribution of what they call unholy reading material. S.N.A.P.spokeswoman Ms.Lee Armstrong said that"since she burned her bra in 1968 she would have no way of protesting this summer except to burn her underwear. An unnamed lesbian rights group has expressed interest in attending this function ,provided that the burning is done on an unwindy day so that they may all get a sniff.The original cause of this big stink(sic)was an article by the American Medical Association stateing that females differ from men because they do not pocess testicles. An official statement from S.N.A.P. retorted indignently... "How dare they say I got no balls,When I get finished with those faggot doctors they wont have any either".

DOWN TO SUNLESS SEA IS FINALLY RELEASED !

The trashey paperback novel of our times has finally hit the news stand in the same way as urriah hits a fan. Unfortunately for the Science Fiction fans who get bombarded by this book the shit hits them. It is most unfortunate that the readers and niave public are not as dead as the armageddon world suggested in this crass pretense for a story. It would be much more fortunate for the public to be blown to nucular oblivian than to have to read this trash. In other and possibly more appropiate words this cheep,discusting,miserable, excuse for a mangey,ignorant,rude and vile piece of turkey dung is not fit to wipe the behind of the lowliest insect which infests the sewers of New York City.The most redeeming feature of this book is that it will surely coax modest literary critics out of seclusion to maintain the dignity of honest Science Fiction writers. All that may be hoped is that(cont'd.).....

When You Piss Upon A Star

--- An Edifying Column By: Count Eric Von Schicklegruber III

Allright, now you've skimmed through this ish of Swill, you can read something of great literary importance: me. Those who can't read may skip this section, until it is released as a movie. Instead you can turn to Lester Lainsford's column and giggle at his warped sense of reality. (What is reality; I dunno.)

Now for the part you've been waiting for; this month's victim. Lemme give you a clue. He is short. And strange. That's right! It's Harlan Ellison, the boy blunder. Why pick on Harlan, you ask. Cause the puke has the nerve to place an add in F&SF selling "The Harlan Collection", where, for a mere several tens of dollars, you get a catalog that lists his records, where he reads his nondescript books. (Thoses who remember AC Clarke reading 2001 on record will recall what a bomb it was. And Clarke was talented. Harlan ain't.) Yes, fans, for only a few hundred pennies, you can get a piece of polyvinyl chloride that goes on a record masher, and emits the squeaky sound of Harlan reading his "fiction" in a monotone voice. And for those fools out there who really want to get rid of your cash, you can actually get Harlan to sign the bloody thing, for a few bucks more. Now I have collected signatures of writers, in my younger days. At one point I even had about ten. Harlan wasn't one. (Well, actually, I lie. I did get him to sign a piece of paper for me. I thought he was Dean Ing. When I decifered the scrawl, I burned the paper. Very satisfying.) Now, what will be the next step? Spider Robinson making sounds on a cassette? Larry Niven groaning on TV? Spare us. And Harlan, sit on the spindle and rotate.

Since Ish No 2, a few hundred people(or less) have wroted to me about my fellow asshole columnist, Lester Lainsford, and his nondescript writing style. They also complain of his order of science. Every one that wrote to me, told me the same thing: of all the sciences, chemistry is the best. Why? Because its there. That's good enough for most. Consider: without chemists, there would be no plastic bags that allow your lunch sandwiches to go soggy and mushy. They would have to wrap new products in paper, instead of plastic wrap. There would be no records, or TV (Phosphorus doesn't grow on trees, ya know), or newspaper (ink is a polymer formula). In short, we would have a lousy life. But without physicists, what would we have...no lack of anything. Physicists are taught to do fuck all in their lives. And that's what they do. Some get paid fantastic amounts of money to do it. For that kind of cash, they should work for Ontario Hydro, where they do even less. By the way, I'm not a physicist. I'm normal.

One writer last week asked about my name, saying that Hitler was a Schicklgruber. Correct, but Hitler had no "e" after the "l". That obviously makes me superior. As for my daddy, old Eric the II, and his dad, Eric the I, and his mother Eric, we are a proud race with no Fascist types whatsoever. So leave me alone you Capitalist morons. Go soak your GNP. Let me read Mein Kampf ist Kaput by myself. Screw off. Eat a lifeboat. Swallow a balloon, then add helium. Fill your mouth with dried prunes, and add water.

See you next ish, maybe.

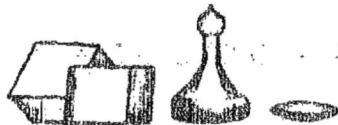

BOARD GAME REVIEW PAGE   By Stephano

Well ,here it is board game fans. This is what you have all been waiting
for. Swill fanzine proudly presents the first annual board game review.
Without further adoo allow me to present in order the greatest games of
all time.

#1. With a five star plus rateing; Ceasar *****
    Ceasar is the greatest board game for one reason. I invented it. Yes,
Science Fiction Fans, this is the perfect combination of strategy, skill,
luck and fun. Indeed had this game been invented but, 2000years earlier
the entire coarse of human history would be different. The Romans would
have stayed home and played this game instead of conquering the world.
At present this game is only available through writing directly to me at;
7 Rollet drive, Toronto, Canada, M6L 1J8. All enquires welcome.

#2. With a stupendous four star rateing, Chess ****
    The attraction of this game is quite understandable. It offers men
the oppertunity to play against those otherwise infalable computors.I
say otherwise because at present a computor has never been programed to
play a perfect game of chess. Well,I sure beat them. For you mediocre
chess players who can't get satisfaction proveing that you are indeed
of superior intellect to the greatest machine;well...youcan always pull
out the plug before it wins.

#3. With a respectable three and a half star rateing, Dungeons and Dragons .
    In this game you and up to ten other people can live out your fantasies
of exploreing a dark dungey dungeon. You can live out your fantasy of meeting
potentially lethal sketatons, zombies and harpies. You can live out your
fantasy of killing cute little fire breathing DRAGONS for experience points.
What? You say that you do not have such fantasies. You say that you are much
more the kindly, good natured non-violent type. Hey, you can be my D.M.!

#4. Ideal for a rainy day in a NorthernOntario cottage. Risk **
    Last time that I played Risk, my best friend ate some lime green risk-
chips by mistake.Well they are the most appitising part of the game.Certainly
there are faster ways of loosing your five best friends than spending three
weeks wipeing them out in a game of risk. If you outright attack someones
continent they may never speak to you again for the rest of your life and
if you don't attack the game will continue so long that you may all begin
suffering the agony of hunger pains. You too may begin to look hungerily at
the appitising little green risk chips.

#5. With one star. (Well, it beats reading trashy Science Fiction).Diplomacy.
    A game where seven people around a table lie, betray,eavesdrop,double-
cross,tripplecross,doubledeal,plot and break alliances and generally behave
as their political counterparts. The game invariably leads to a popularity
contest in which the most scrupulous person is attacked first and the most
cunningly discusting player survives as the victor. If you can leave your
scruples at home you will love it! With seven players Turkey"s aim will be
to survive three turns;Russia's aim to dissimate Turkey;Austria-Hungary's
aim to destroy Italy;while Italy must somehow ally with Austria-Hungary,it's
agressor;A Franco-Russian pact assures France success against Italy;To survive,Germany must eliminate one country immediately,preferably France;The
island of England is strongest defensively but,experience confirms that it
requires at least two strong allies before it attacks anyone successfully.
These suggestions should steadfastly be obeyed unless Italy makes a pass at
your girlfriend,France gets drunk or Germany insults you with a racial slur.

BUK RIVOOS

by Illy Literate

HITCHHIKERS GUIDE TO BRAMALEA Uglass Dams, Panned Books, $3.95
     This tome is worth buying. It details the adventures of a fellow
who is taken by a nasty person on a trip through Bramalea. Numerous
horrors are encountered on the way. After a trip in a garbage scow,
they are ejected into the middle of Highway 3, where, luckily, a
passing SPCA truck picks them up before they die of boredom. The
truck is driven by a madman who resembles Bill Davis, in search of
relection. Upon entering Bramalea, they encounter superior beings
from Ottawa who have been alive for decades, who explain how Bramalea
was constructed as an experiment in Futility, in search of the
answer for it all. Turns out the answer is delivered on the top
of Mt. Chinguacousy (really!) when the hero is run over by a speeding
dial-a-bus driven by Stuart Smith. I highly reccommend this buk as
worth stealing, buying, or otherwise obtaining.

EXPANDED BALLOON Robert A Lowlife, Dorkley Books, $3.75
     Rehash of previous useless book, with many extra words added for
filling. Title page is nicely done, as is the back cover. Nothing
else of note.

RINGWORM ENGINEERS Loose Women, Barter Boks, $2.50
     Story of a psWychopathic veterinarian who steals a million dollars
from the Royal Mint and begins genetic engineering project on a
new resilient strain of ringworm. After falling with a cat-creature,
he constructs a species that bites its own tail, and begins to
eat untill it digests itself. Amusing tail, worth reading.

347 THINGS TO DO WITH A RUBBER STOPPER (2nd Ed.)
     See last issue for original review. This second edition adds
pictures to make the enjoyment of using a rubber stopper even better.
Picture of Rubber Stopper being used as a constipation aid is especially
informative. If you haven't got the first edition, get this one.

THE MAD ELEPHANT THAT ATE BETELGEUSE Anonymous, Toilet Bux, 75c
     Excellent for those rainy nights when you can't think of any-
thing to do. Details the story of a mad elephant that gets transported
to Betelgeuse, where a magician steps on his trunk. In a rage, the
elephant eats the planet. Descriptions of the munching sounds as the
elephant eats the mantle are very vivid. This will be followed by
a sequel next year that continues the tale of the elephant shit that
was Betelgeuse.

THE BEST OF HARLAN ELLISON Harlan Ellison, Ripoff Pubs, 7.50
     This is undoubtedly the best thing Ellison has ever done. The
over three hundred pages are all blank. Especiallywell suited for
those who can't read, and looks impressive on the shelf. Ellison
will not be able to top this one.

DUNE, CONTINUED Frank Herbert, Prentice Hull, 12.98
     Yet another of the unbelieveable Dunes series. This one is
probably the best of the lot. It makes an excellent door stop.

THE GODS THEMSELVES Isick Asimov, Afun, 2.50

Marginal Phun   By JR

- I hear that OSFIC is holding a con at the Holiday Inn. But that's no suprise.

- Dating Nuns is a bad habit.

- There once was a country in the Orient that was ruled by the Great Shan. Now the Shan was a great man, but he had one small little problem, ie: he was epileptic. There for he had a personal physician. But one day it happened, the doctor was away at a seminar, and the Shan had a seizure. That night the doctor returned, and was met at the gate by the palace gaurd. Now the gaurd was mad, the doctor was supposed to be there when the Shan had his attackes, and he wasn't. So the gaurd yelled to the Doctor at the top of his lungs,"Where were You when the fit hit the Shan."

- John went to his Doctor. "Hay Doc I have a problem,every time I fart my farts sound like Honda."

Dr. Hung looked at John and said,"Sorry I can't do anything for you. But I know someone who can. Go see your Dentist."

"What."

"Just go see him," Dr,Hung said.

So John went to his dentist, who found an abscess. The dentist fixed this. John was glad, but he went back to his Doctor to find out why. When John asked Dr.Hung how the abscess caused his condition, the Doctor replied," Abscess makes the fart go Honda."

Dear Swill

I am protesting about an aricle you taste-less slobs thought fit to publish. The artical That is a gross misrepresentation is on found in that FILTHY DISGUSING thing you call litriture. This is of cource No. 1.The article in question is Trash and the Trekkie ,or should I say trash! It implies that there are only two personel in the Canadian armed force.(farce). This is dead wrong. I know I'm a slave of this astablishment? Thre there are more than two prisons in the force. Why there's a General Fuckup, General Disorder, Major Nucance, Major Catastrophy and I once heard of a Colonel O.F. Corn. Then ,of cource theres me.

                           Yours

                        Private Parts

        Okay, all ready. We stand corrected. Still, you've got
  to admit that the armed farces which you state contains six people(?)
  is somewhat smaller than the Royal Canadian Air Farce. By the way,
  when did we ever call SWILL litriture? (That's literature, illiterate!)

VOOOOOOOOOOOOOOOOOOOSH!

Your majesty:
              So hi! Your masterpiece SWILL got rave reviews here in
  the states. Truely the greatest publication of our times! A stroke of
  genius! Pure art! Magnificent! Tremendous! Sure to change the course of
  literary destiny! Shakespear couldn't have done better! (Okay, enough.
  No need to give you a swolled/head swilled head.

                              Their Gracious Vooshing Majesties:
                              Kurt & Rainbow Kohl
                              Royal Oak, Michigan.

        I have no comment to make on such a touching, truthful,
  and divinely enlightened letter.   ed.

ENDNOTE

An anouncement: as of next issue there will be a change in SWILL. Ie. there will be two editions of SWILL, an eastern and western edition. DON'T PANIC!!! Your favourite pieces will be contained in both issues. My editorial, Pissing on a Pile of Old Amazings, the Buk Revoo, and My Fame shall appear in both editions. SO DON'T WORRY! We'll also probabley include whatever we deen to be the feature article too.

Why this change in policy? Well, I'm moving to ultra-WONDERFUL british columbia. Therefore, Arne Hanaver is going to take over the the editorship of the eastern edition. Though I'll still remain editor-in-Chief. Arne is well qualified to take over this post. He has been published in such magazines as Reticulum and Sirius, and is WONDERFUL. And thus he now has the eastern editorship post. I will be the editor of the western edition.

So I hope you'll enjoy both editions of SWILL. They will be ~~avail~~ availabel in both eastern and western areas. Tell us which one you like best.

So that's about it. So much for the announcemrent.

So you find the editorial too political. Well tough shit!!!! That's the way things are.

SWILL $1.00 Canadian $1.25 American   Subscriptions $8.00 per year

NIEL _____

(GONE TO BC) SEE YOU

AT V-COU

Peter

Thanks Pete! I
always enjoy a printers
strike. Too bad you
couldn't stay to finish
running off the issue

04.7
58
Sh.1
01.2

Me + Asra'll just drink the
rest of your scotch. See you at V-Cu

SUPRISE!

YOUR SWILL HAS ARRIVED

You have received this wonder of literary excellance
BECAUSE:

☐ We think you'll like it.
☐ We know you'll hate it. (tough shit!)
☐ You are a depraved wacko.
☐ You contributed to it. (Use the toilet next time!!!)
☐ You bought it. (Dummy)
☐ You sububscribe to it. (You're even dumber!)
☐ You are wonderful, maybe.
    (Note: only we are WONDERFUL!!!!!!)

SWILL RULES O.K.!!!

SWILL #4.5

August 1981

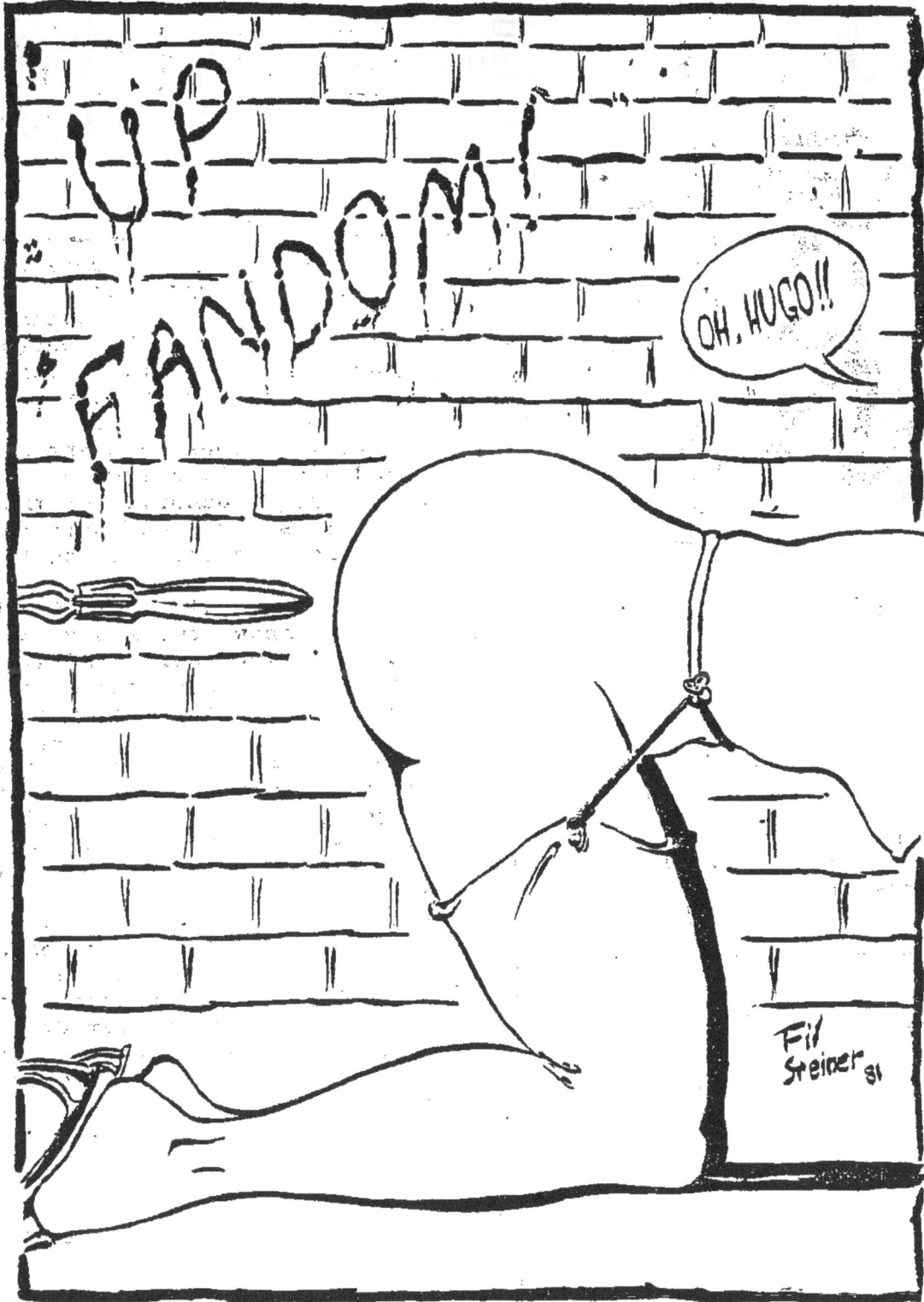

SWILL

SPECIAL "WORLDCON" ISSUE

CONTRIBUTERS

Neil Williams
Stephano
Fil Steiner
Illy Litrate

SWILL MAGAZINE
Volume #1, Number #4B
August 1981
© 1981 Vile Fen Press

SWILL Logo by Kevin Davies
Editorial Title by
        Grant Emon

SWILL MAGAZINE
Suite 116
335 E. Broadway
Vancouver, B.C.
V5T 1W5.

SWILL MAGAZINE is owned
and opperated by V.P.Press
AN ALL CANADAIN COMPANY

EDITORIAL

Welcome to the 1981 Worldcon, folks.
Worldcon?? Well, not quite. Actually
Americon would be a more fitting title
for this convention. The "Worldcon" has
always had a heavy American influence
and although, in recent years, we've
seen more "Worldcons" outside of the U.S.
the majority of these conventions have
been, and are still being, held within
the territorial boundries of the U.S.
And so this is why I dub this convention,
Americon since, after all, that is what
it really is.

Why is this so? To be truthful, I
really don't know, but I have a theory
nonetheless. The "Worldcon" started in
the States. It was nurtured in the U.S.
and the majority of the conventioners
were from the U.S. Therefore, logically,
if you are an American what convention
bid are you going to vote for, one that
you're going to have to fly 4,000 kilo-
metres to get to or one that may be only
a few hours drive away? Not only that
but are you going to vote for a con in a
foreign country where they may not speak
English or have odd customs, or are you
going to vote for the con that is in the
good ol'e US of A, where the host city is
not all that different from Cypress
Corners, Iowa? If you're an American
you'd vote for the American convention,
right? Right.

Of course, foreign "Worldcon" bids
also face another problem---unfair competition. The dice are loaded for the
American bids. "Bullshit!" you say.
Well, bullshit to you too. Look, chances
are that the con you're going to be bidding
at is going to be held in the U.S., correct? Therefore, most of the people who
will be attending that convention will
also be American, right? And what does

CONTINUED --------------

EDITORIAL CONTINUED

that mean? It means that the American bid is able to drum up support within the U.S. at very little cost. Someone on the committee is going to such-and-such a con. Great, give him a budget to hold a room party to advertise the American bid. In the past, compeating with such advertising methods has been impossible for foreign worldcon bids. They have just caught on to a way to combat this, by having American agents for their bids.

I am referring to the work done by the Australia in '83 committee. The Aussies have agents for their bid who have been attending U.S. conventions to gather support. It has been an admirable effort, though I believe that it has also been a costly effort, too. Surely it has cost the Aussies more to gain the support that they have than it has cost Baltimore. The results of this effort will be discovered this weekend, and I sincerely hope that the Aussies win, since they are the bid that truely deserves to.

Which brings me to another point, Baltimore's trump card. Obviously the problem of having some real competition from a foreign bid has truely worried Baltimore, forcing them to use their ace. Baltimore won't hold a Northamericon if they lose the "Worldcon" bid. How childish! It is a definite blow below the belt. It is nasty and uncalled for, but it quite possibly may be the winning card in this bidding war. And it is precisely this stunt which has convinced me not to even consider, even remotely nurish the thought of voting for Baltimore. But as things appear at the moment, I think that the sniveling whiners of Baltimore will regretably win their bid.

So you see, the "Worldcon" is really America's national S.F. convention. It is not in any real sense an international event. It is only the largest annual convention(s.f.) held in the world, I believe(I have to check some figures with some Japanese fan to be certain).

What about the Hugos, you may protest. What about them? They're America's science fiction awards for excellance in the genre. Look at the average Hugo ballot, the majority, if not all of the books, ect. are by American authors. Why? Because most of the nominations and votes are from American fans, the majority of which read only American s.f. So even the Hugos aren't really international awards. They are just simply American awards.

Well, I hope that I haven't upset you too much by my small attack on one of the sacred cows of fandom. And, in conclusion, I sincerely hope that you enjoy yourself at Denvention 2, the 39th annual Americon.

Neil Williams

BUK RIVOO

my edertur reasently told
me to rite a rivoo on three uf
the buks up for the 1981 yugo
award. the buks he sujested wer
beyond the blew event whorizin,
the ringwirld enginears, and lord
valentines cassil. I bot thees
buks and tried to reed then so I
culd tell you aboyt them
hear is the rivoo.

beyond the blu event whorizin
this wuz an eezee buk to
reed it wuz not to complikayted
i culd realy identify with the
karactors and i liked the senes
put in for sexual arowsment. just
like in the movies. this is my
choyss for best buk.

the ringwild enginears
this wuzent a bad buk but
it was hard too reed. ther wuz
sum sience stuf that i didn't
understand. the characyors wer
not eezee to identfy with cuz to
of them wer alians. this is a
sort uf interesting buk it is
my second choys.

lord valintines cassil
i didn't like this buk at
all it wuz two complikayed.
the riter used lots of big words
that i didn't kno. it is also a
long buk. i culd not finish it
the karactors wer not like peopl
i kno. i culd not identify with
them. they had too much stuff
going thru their heads. this buk
makes a good doorstop: ILLY LITRATE

ENDNOTE

Well I hope you've enjoyed
this short issue of SWILL. We'-
ve had a few problems the past
few months, particularly in the
area of communications. I moved
out to the west coast, and then
the mail strike hit. What a
bloody mess! Issue #5 is, to my
knowledge, still somewhere within the Canadian postal system.
Whether it shall ever surface is
something that I really don't
know. Perhaps it might. Issue
#6 was stalled due to lack of
articles, and what you are now
reading was supposed to be issue
#7, but we had to trim it down
consuderably, so you only have
a #4B. As you can see, we've
had a few setbacks, to say the
least.
But, the mails are moving
again and SWILL#5 will appear at
the end of September. It will
be the satandard 14 pages in
length. It will also contain all
the regular features that you
have come to know and enjoy, my
wonderful editorial, Lester's
illustrious column, the Hoyt
column, Illy's "Buk Rivoo", and
the MY FAME comic strip. Plus
there will be some new features
and a brand new, second comic
strip to fill up extra spaces
at the bottom of some page. All
in all, it's going to be a great
ish. Don't miss the triumphant
return of SWILL!

Neil Williams: Editor-in-Chief

THE SAGA OF MY FAME

...AN SO IT WAS BORN!

WORLD CON 81

DID YOU LIKE THIS MONTH'S FRONT COVER? If you did, you can now get it on a T-shirt. Neat, eh? For your special "UP FANDOM" T-shirt send one $7.00 money order, plus your name, address, and postal code, and shirt size to: SWILL MAGAZINE Suite 116, 335 E. Broadway, Vancouver, B.C., CANADA, V5T 1W5.

SWILL #5

September 1981

Swill

Volume One
Number 5
$1.00

™

JWFraser '81

1

SWiLL

SEPT. 81, Volume #1, Number #5, Whole # 6.

CONTRIBUTERS

Neil Williams
Stephano
Andrew Hoyt
David White
Reginold Planetage
Ruby Beroach

SWILL MAGAZINE
Volume #1, Number##5
September 1981
c 1981 Vile Fen Press

SWILL logo by Kevin
                 Davies
Editorial logo by Grant
                 Emon

SWILL MAGAZINE
#206, 3570 E. Hastings
Vancouver, B.C,
V5R-2A7.

Cover by Vaughn Fraser

EDITORIAL

VIVA, MAPLECON!

As I write this month's editorial, it is fast approaching that time of the year when Ottawa fandom holds its own regional convention, Maplecon. Maplecon has a special place in the heart of this magazine, since(unbeknownst to its con committee) it is solely responsible for the idea of SWILL. Without Maplecon there would be no SWILL and fans would be deprived of a major source of toilet paper. This is how it all began, sorta.

One evening in October of last year, a few days before Maplecon 3, Lester and I decided we were going to do something for the con. What, we hadn't yet got around to deciding. I bounced a few ideas off of Lester, none of which he liked. That is until I mentioned the Detroit "Boycott Chicago in '82" campain. Lester liked that, and a couple of hours later, the "Imfamous Maplecon 3 Slandersheet" emerged from my typewriter. The slandersheet was run off and copies were distributed at the con, much to the dismay of the con committee. Oh, well.

But the slandersheet also gave rise to the idea of producing a nasty, one-shot fanzine for the worldcon, called: UP FANDOM. We made all sorts of plans for the 'zine, articles, the cover, ect. It was going to be really controversial. (It still will be, when it comes out, Date still to be announced.)

Well, a couple of months went by, Lester was trying to improve his score on a video game called "Missle Command" and I was working on producing a perzine. UP FANDOM sat on the back burner until news about the slandersheet began to leak out of Ottawa.

Ottawa fandom, it seems, was rather

annoyed about the slandersheet. In true fannish tradition, the rumours abounded. Maplecon was suposed to be sueing for libel. OSFiC (Ontario Science Fiction Club) was suposed to be suing for misrepresentation. The authors of the slandersheet had suposedly been found and were going to be dealt with in a non legal fashion. Seriously dealt with. All these rumours were unfounded, of course. Still we laid low for a couple of months just to make sure.

But as January came about and I still hadn't produced a fanzine, I got an idea. I decided to do a one-shot nastyzine as a trial run for UP FANDOM. Lester agreed and in February SWILL #1 appeared. It was to be a one-shot, but certain things developed. It was warmly recieved by the students of York University, which both of us attended.

In particular, we began to recieve material from one student named Stephano. Lots and lots of material. At present, I still have enough Stephano material to do an entire, full sized SWILL containing nothing but Stephano. In light of this development, I put out another issue of SWILL, and have(barring the communications breakdown due to the postal strike) continued to put out an issue every month since.

So Maplecon is rather special to us here at SWILL I have attended two of the three Maplecons that have been held to date. I enjoyed the fi first one, but Maplecon 3 was a great disappointment. It was as the slandersheet describes (see inside back cover of this issue) a comics con, not a SF con. But it appears that this year's con committee has learned from the errors of last year's disaster. From the fourth hand reports I'm recieving out of Ottawa. It appears that this year's con will most definitely be a Science Fiction con. Steps have been made to curtail the numbers of dealers at the con. In fact, the red tape and restrictions on dealers at Maplecon 4 are as sound as any by the federal government on foreign investment. Thus, I doubt that there will be any dealers from outside of Ottawa at the convention. This is fantastic because it will halt the number of grubby little prepubescent munchkins that'll show up at the convention. It'll also cut down the number of mediafen and overweight Trekkies at the con too. Plus, I here that they will have a con suite this year.(They didn't really have one last year.) Maplecon 4, seems to have returned to the stage it was at after Maplecon 2. Comics have been returned to their rightful, inferior place, in the natural order of things.

So thanks Maplecon, and good luck this year. Sorry, but I'm not attending. It's too far and I don't trust prophecies based on 4th hand info.(even my own).

neil williams

PISSING ON A PILE OF OLD AMAZINGS

...a modest column
by Lester Rainsford

(Still lost within the bowels of the Canadian Postal system. ed.)

BUK RIVOO

by Illy Litrate

(Suffering the same fate as Lester's column. ed.)

THE THREAT FROM BELOW

A GUEST COLUMN
by David White

Readers of sf, unite. Help stamp out the biggest threat to us, we know of. I'm referring to the assinine cretins known as teenage fans. Theses little twerps tend to do nasty things that give the rest of us a bad name. It's not enough that when I go into my favourite sf. bookstore that I have to shoulder my way through hundreds of pimply, fat munchkins, but when I see the last copy of a book I want and reach for it, one of these twerps always places its grubby paws on it first. Then it stands around till I leave, and replaces it. These assholes of the miniature variety have little cash to spend, so they read the fucking books in the store, leaning on the counter, or squatting on the floor. They make it as difficult as possible to get past them. These little herds of turds also seem to crop up where-ever I go. If I lower myself to taking public transit, these cruddos choose to sit behind me and natter in top voice about how "wonderful" the latest Star Drek novel is, and how it typifies sf. Then they turn the conversation to the sf. masterpiece (in their puny minds) Star Bores, and explain how Lucas managed to single-handedly bring decent sf. to the screen. As for classics like 2001, that's below their dignity, as it is older t than they, and as such is vintage. Well, I say we should exterminate all the little fuckers! If we wipe out all the under 18 fans, we will hve no worries. They will cease to bother us. So next time you see a myopic, pimpled twerp reading The Gods Themselves, stick your foot through its eyes!

THE SHAPE OF THINGS THAT ARE

a short, but nevertheless absorbing column
by Andrew Hoyt

How do I hate Star Wars. Let me count the ways. I hate the way starships rumble in the vacuum of space. I hate the way light energy weapons have a backfire. I hate the way ships whip from one star system to another in a matter of minutes. I hate the expression of supralight speed. I hate the way effects have stars doplering the wrong way. I hate the way ground based fighters simply jump into space and fly around at great velocities. I hate the way people build robots that can only be understood by another robot. I hate the way actors never stop to eat or drink (except in a bar). I hate the way the man in the plastic mask sounds like he's speaking though a reperator, even if he is. I hate the way spaceships have no toilets. I hate the way storm

CONTINUED ON PAGE 6

4

READERS BEWARE!

a guest book review
by Reginold Planetage

The Book of Vile Darkness, by Unknown Authors, compiled by A. Rogers, published by Van-Sham Press, Toronto, 1982 release (275 pages; hardcover).

"This mystic text contains much of the arcane knowledge of midiev#1 myth, magic, and folklore. Bound in impressive black leatherette with gold trim, this compilation is a curious addition to any 'Librum'. Chapters one through four on the subject of ineffable damnation require study of a period of no less than a week to glean this most chaotic exaltation!"
THE TORONTO SON

In all fairness to this book, one must answer the question of whether the text is worth reading. The criteria which must be used is, the effect of The Book of Vile Darkness upon the reader. What will the reader learn from the book and/or how will he be differant after reading it?
The following statistics give the approximate reader response of 100 Book of the Month Club subscribers whom were mailed a copy of the text, at random, as part of a publishers' survey.

3% of the readers suffered no ill effects whatsoever.
19% of the readers incurred a criminal record within one day of recieving the book.
20% of the readers reported horrible nightmares and occult experiences.
25% of the readers were driven totally insaine.
35% of the readers went into a coma for three to five

days, and of the people in a coma, roughly half died a tormented death while the other half recovered to report that they had thoroughly enjoyed the book.

Of the survivors, those who read past chapter five were shocked to discover that their hair had turned totally white, that they had lost all intrest in sex, that any metal objects that they touched began to rust instantly, and that they had an uncontrolable urge to preform a ritual blood sacrifice of the family house pet.

The one reader who managed to get past chapter six of the text noticed a hairy wart-like growth on his lower lip had formed and that he'd began to grow a long tail-like appendage. He chanted uncontrolably until his death, ten minutes later.

RESERVE your copy of The Book of Vile Darkness NOW! Just send $9.99 to Van-Sham Press, 4266 Bloor St. W., Toronto, Ont., CANADA. (Makes a fine Xmas gift!)

AFTER THE "WORLDCON"

Earlier this month(Sept.) I attended the "Worldcon" in Denver, U.S.A. I have to admit that I had an excellant time at the con. I saw some old friends, made some new ones, and generally had a lot of fun. Of course, I also had a lot of negative feedback on the editorial that appeared in last month's ish, which was distributed at the con.

The editorial postulated that the "Worldcon" should more aptly be titled Americon, since it is the American's national convention. Well, I still hold to that opinion. I talked to a lot of fen at the con on this subject and it hasn't shaken my opinion one milimetre. (Though I do take back all my comments on the nastiness of the Baltimore in '83 bidding committee. They are not at all the anti-foreign fen devils I made them out to be.)

Still, the "Worldcon" is just an Americon. Of the 39 "Worldcons" held to date, only seven of them have been held outside of the U.S.A. Two of these were held here in Canada. Thus, only five "Worldcons" have been held outside on North America, and only one has been held in a non-English speaking country (Heidelberg in 1970.) Yet American fans still insist that their national convention is a "Worldcon".

At Denvention II, I met a lot of fen from many nations. Australia, Britain, Europe, Japan, and South East Asia. There were even fans from Africa, though I didn't run into them. The fact that so many fans from different countries attend the "Worldcon" is one of the reasons that the Americans insist that it is a Worldcon.

But, the International science confrences are not held in one country predominantly, they travel all over the globe. So shouldn't our "international" confrence do the same, at least once every four years? Should the four year rotation ever get passed into the Worldcon const-itution, we will then have a true Worldcon. But until that day, a real Worldcon does not yet exist, except in name, though not in spirit.

Neil Williams

Andrew Hoyt (continued from page 4)

troopers' armour explodes in a flash of magnesium, while rebels' cloth withstands supernovas. I hate the way Leia Orgasma always has makeup on. I hate phoney-looking aliens. I hate little green aliens that sound like Grover and Fozzie rolled into one. I hate light sabers that automatically end at a certain length, and make a stupid buzzing sound. I hate the way hands are bionically replaced, and yet less serious wounds are left to kill. I hate planet exploding beams that come from a dish ariel. I hate convenient little entrance hatches that destroy great big ships. I hate the force. I hate carbon encoating suspension materials. I hate reaction engines that have no reaction. I hate automatic gravity. I hate planets that support life, and creatures that live in asteroids. I love the fucking movies.

Below: a new SWILL comic strip.

THE ADVENTURES OF STAR CAPTAIN BRUCE

LOCS (letters of coment)

Due to the mail strike,
I only have some old locs this
ish. They are all from the
same person(?). Two arrived
before the strike and the other two arrived just after the
strike. They are not wonderful, but here goes anyway.

Sir Swill,
Between marijuanna
harvests on our commune there
is not much to do, so I fill
my time balling my girl-friend
Sarrah, reading Swill, and
fixing my old blue jeans. I
like SWILL cuz it makes great
patches for my old blue jeans.
Ruby Beroach
(Last of the Hip-
pies.)

uh-huh? an interesting
application there. but what
happens if you get caught in
the rain, or horrors of horrors, wash your clothes? ed.

Sir Swill,
I dig rock and roll
music, sex, good Nepanese Hash,
and Swill. I was rapping with
my friends at the commune and
there is just one thing that
we don't get. How come you
charge money for Swill, man?
Did you sell out to the system?
Don't you believe in free Swill
man?

Ruby Beroach

free swill? look man, we
charge a buck when we can get
it, 50¢ otherwise. most of h
the copies are traded or given
away. like, have you ever had
to pay for one yet, man???

Sir Swill,
I was spaced out in a
Loblaws supermarket the other
day when I suddenly experianced

a revelation. Like wow man!!!
I found myself reading Swill,
issue #4. Far fucking out, man.
I suddenly realised the meaning of
the cover man. (the cover said:
ONE SWILL--12 GRAMS--New). I med-
itated on this really good Columbian pot and the cover sent this
message to me...and the cosmos.
The cover said...(Are you ready
for this, man?)...it said...(okay,
don't get your pee hot)...it said
...(Is this magazine bugged by the
R.C.M.P. narcs, man?)..I'll tell
you what it said, soon as I light
up another spliff.
Oh wow, my eyes are burning!
I am electric in outer space! I'll
tell you what the cover said now.
But, before I knew it I had smoked
all twelve grams of the Swill and
had forgotten what it had said.
That is a bummer, but like wow, I
gotta say that this Swill shit is
a real good high!!!!
Ruby Beroach

(Hey man, like no comment.
like, i'm stoned myself and this
has gotta go to press in the morning. ed.)

The hell with the Endnote. This is
the Endnote. SWILL lives and I
am wonderful, I think, maybe.
Blorts and nurkles. ed.

PORTRAIT OF A PUNK ARTIST By AhFasor

SUPPORT SCIENCE FICTION READER'S RIGHTS! BOYCOTT MAPLECON III!

Every year, true science fiction fans are degraded by the travesty of a 'sf convention' mounted by an incestuous unholy alliance of ottawa pseudo-fans and comic book fanatics. This farce of a money-grubbing grasp for our money is solely designed to enrich the pockets of of stupid slothbrained comic book collectors who use this ill-beggoten gains to buy more of their puraile little picture books with stories for morons who read out XXXXX. lua.

Why do true sf fans have to put up with twits who think superman and batshit and the rest of the fucking horde   are up there in litrary merit with EE Smith and Leguin and the rest of the sf greats? Why must true sf fans have to listen to eager beaver dipshit talks about Green Hornet wants to screw Robin??   Or does wonder woman use vibrating tampons???

F urthermore, there is also at this convention a dealers section. These dealers, who sometimes have the idiotic idea that they are sf 'fans', are really one of the biggest assholes to screw true sf fans that there is.

Have you ever tried to buy a used used book? You know what outrageous profiteering prices these leeches charge for even torn copies of Ivor Jorgensons Ten From Infinity? A cocksucker book if there ever was one? Go to Bakka books in Torontso and try to buy a copy of niven's Shape of space. Just try to. Why are used books so expensive? Because it is a plot!!! A fucking ploy by assholes who try to get rid of their useless old paperbacks, and want more money!!! These capitalist swine rip-off the true sf fan by denying the true sf fan many old good books. Alas, many used sf bookstores run by these leeches sell comic books, thus perpetuating this swinish breed.

Look, if you are a true sf fan, why dont you leave now and let the rest of the fairies a screw themselves in the ass and jerk off over Green Hornet in heroic poses? Let the bastafd fucking toad-spawn be fed to chickens!! Stnd up for sf rights!!!

Sincerely yours, The Ontario Scince Fiction Association
                                                club
                                            the motherfuckers

(A paid fen-political announcement)

SWILL #6

December 1981

reconstructed version

SWILL

Volume 1   Number 6

SWILL

SWILL
Volume 1, Number 6
December 1981

c 1981/2024 Vile Fen
Press

SWILL Logo
Kevin Davies

Editorial Logo
Grant Emon

Cover
Hormel Marketing

Back Cover
Kevin Davies

CONTRIBUTORS
Neil Williams

Please Stand By

Unlike the case of Daughter of Swill, Mother of Scum: third trimester -- I have little recollection as to what was the content of SWILL #6. Only this: it had a cover by a Vancouver fan artist whose name I cannot remember, the editorial was about Christmas, it contained two to three Star Captain Bruce comic strips, had a book review and a film review. The print run was small, maybe 200 copies, probably only 150, and I would have only brought about forty to fifty copies to the 1981 "BasKon" New Year's Party in Toronto.

This is NOT going to be a reconstruction, at all. This will be vague re-creation based on a couple of scraps of memory and little else. So, maybe (just maybe) 10% actual recollection, 30% re-creation, and 60% complete fiction (that is, a total fabrication of what might have been in the issue).

I am also, as I did for Daughter of Swill, Mother of Scum: third trimester, going to attempt to cast my mind back in time and write SWILL #6 as if I was 45 years younger. This may not work as well (and I am not certain that it worked there either...).

On Christmas

I really don't know where I am
with Christmas. I am not a
believer. I am also not an
atheist. I am not an agnostic
either. I am pretty certain
that there is some sort of
Supreme Being, but I am also
certain that It is not
humancentric. I do not see
this Being, spending all of
Its time keeping an eye on
this little planet, Earth.
The universe is absolutely
massive (and probably a series
of nested multiverses) and we
humans are NOT the fucking
centre of everything. We are
NOT "made in God's image"
other than we are sentient and
have a consciousness (and
also, I believe, a soul). In
the grand scheme of things, we
humans are minor players,
extras, perhaps we are just a
"side show".

Someone I know, quipped the
other day, "Jesus is the
reason for the season." He is
very religious of the
evangelical Protestant

variety. He believes that the
Earth is only 10,000 years
old, that humans and dinosuars
existed at the same time, that
there is no evolution, and
each of us were hand-crafted
by God. I don't buy any of
that. Look I got myself into
trouble in Roman Catholic
Sunday School, as the leading
priest and all of the "old
people" (that meant to my ten
year-old self anyone over
forty) who taught Sunday
School were all of

a pre-Vatican II mindset;
human evolution did NOT occur.
I found this difficult. That
was because, back then,
natural evolution of the
cosmos, of stars, and planets,
and basic life could be
attributed to being the
handiwork of God or to follow
Natural Laws (created by and
initiated by God). Humans,
however, were the definite
work of God. There were no
questions regarding that. I
found it hypocritical that the
Church was fine with evolution
following Natural Law, which
had been created by and
initiated by God, except when
it came down to human beings.
My co-worker in 1981 who was
an evangelical Protestant is
more rationally honest; the
entire scientific worldview is
wrong and only the literal

Biblical Christian worldview is correct.

And if "Jesus is the reason for the season"; then why?? Is it because he was a wonderful preacher? I can accept that. Or is it because He is the "Son of God" who was born to "die for our sin" and is a "sacrifice" to attain forgiveness for humanity for "original sin". Because I have a big fucking problem with that one.

So, we have the original humans, Adam and Eve living in the Garden of Eden where they are pure, and ignorant, and living in a state of bliss. God has told them not to eat the fruit of the Tree of Knowledge and they did; this wiped out their innocence and bliss and inflicted upon them death (they would now age and die) and original sin that all humans will now be born with. God, who is all-powerful and all-knowing has created this scenario, knowing what the humans He has created are going to do, makes no effort to stop them (because they have free will), insists on punishing them when they transgress His rule, and is

incapable of forgiving them (even though He is all-powerful). There is only one hope for humankind, one way to make things right. God must incarnate Himself in human form (as God the Son) and live a human life, then He must be crucified as a sacrifice to Himself (God the Father) as the only sacrifice worthy enough to atone for humanity's original sin, that His death will now "wash away". This is seriously fucked up and a nonsensical blood sacrifice "fairy story", that only has a message of joy for a classical or medieval worldview. To a modern worldview, it is crazy, nutbar thinking.

My evangelical co-worker also doesn't celebrate Christmas with all of the things we associate with Christmas. Their Christmas tree is lit, but without ornaments. There are no Christmas stockings. There is no Santa Claus. Everyone just gets one gift. The focus is on attending church and prayer. He tells me that most of the traditions that are associated with Christmas are evil Pagan traditions. And I am aware of some of these, the date of the birth of Jesus being December 25th is a borrowing from the

4

Roman holiday Saturnalia (Jesus would have actually been born in the late spring or early summer -- late May to mid June) as is the tradition of giving gifts. The Christmas tree comes from the Yule tree of the Pagan Norse and Germanic cultures. And so on...

What is the true meaning of Christmas? Is it to celebrate the observed date of the birth of a remarkable Jewish sage from 2000 years ago? Or is it the observed date of the birth of God incarnated as a human, so that He can grow up to be a blood sacrifice to Himself? or is it something else?

Living in a northern climate, I am going with the something else. Something social and thus human. As the days grow shorter, we gather together on (or around) the shortest day and the longest night of the year. We gather to celebrate community. To celebrate family. To share food and drink and gifts. We do this as the winter is hard, and some of us will not survive to see the spring. We rejoice in being human, in the love we have for each other, and shout

out our resilience, and hold each other close for reassurance, and remember that we are us. Only human. And only people.

We are not the centre of all things. Which is humbling. And, at the same time, we ARE the centre of all things. Our consciousness brings thought to this little planet. We are the people of Earth, a speck in a vast cosmos. And that makes us unique and it also makes us special; we are the only ones who are us.

So for me, Christmas is about gathering together with friends and family. Christmas is about being with family (however you decide to frame that).

Viewing Some Crap

I know that I watched more than two movies in 1981, but at present only two come to mind with any sharp recollection. Those films are "Heavy Metal" and "Outland".

I have never been a fan of Heavy Metal magazine. Still,

on occasion, I would purchase an issue. If one of the serialised graphic novels interested me, I may seek out the earlier segments in previous issues or wait for it to be published in its entirety. I appreciate the art form, but it is not my favourite form of storytelling.

Thus, I was pretty certain what to expect going to the cinema to watch "Heavy Metal". Overall, I was not disappointed (though for one segment I was massively disappointed). As I said, I am not a regular reader of Heavy Metal, I am not devoted to the magazine, nor am I a follower of any particular artist that frequented the pages of the magazine. Thus, I had little invested in the magazine and in the film adaptation. Or so I thought.

The film portrayed classic serials and stories from the magazine. For most, I was either only vaguely familiar with or not at all. Thus, the film adaption neither upset me or inspired me to want more. So, overall, a good job. The green orb of evil serves to link the various tales. However, the film really blows it with their adaption of the Angus McKie graphic novel "So Beautiful and So Dangerous".

There must have been something passing through the zietgeist in the late 1970s that would cause the muses to inspire both "So Beautiful and So Dangerous" and "The Hitchhiker's Guide to the Galaxy". The graphic novel is a shorter work than the original Hitchhiker's radio series and is darker (somewhat) and more philosophical. The tone wavers from humour to very serious, and has a general darker tone than Hitchhiker's; Hitchhiker's careens from the absurd to the mocking to the ethnographic to the sometimes serious.

But, the opening portion of the McKie graphic novel that was adapted as a segment within the film "Heavy Metal", loses most of the tone and most of the context of the original work. It is reduced to being a segment that focuses on sex, boobs, and snorting large quantities of an alien version of cocaine.

It is entertaining and silly;
it captures some of the visual
tone of the original, but not
its core. So, this is a fail
for me.

But, I do give the film 7 out
of 10.

"Outland" is a space western.
It fits the "western" genre as
it is set in an isolated
mining town, surrounded by a
hostile environment, that is
"governed" by a corporation
(aka it is a company town),
and mine workers are
mysteriously dying. And we
have Sean Connery as the newly
stationed Federal Marshall,
William O'Neil there to save
the day. Some people say that
"Outland" is a homage to the
1952 film "High Noon"; I can
see this, but the film is more
than just a re-telling of
"High Noon" in space. There
is also the elements of a
thriller in "Outland", the
mystery of the miner's death
that has to be solved. But,
the "western" genre elements
are strong.

The film is mostly a Western,
in part a Thriller, and
definitely Science Fiction.

It has a strong parallel to
the 1979 film "Alien" in the
design of the mining outpost;
akin to the human ship
Nostromo, a design that is
industrial, pragmatic, and
lacking any soul. And the
heroes and villains are all
just workers (even the local
Management) here on Io for the
high pay, risk bonus, and
potential productivity
bonuses. These are not people
who are on Io to build a brave
new world or expand humanity's
reach on the cosmos; they are
working in a remote and
dangerous location on a one
year contract for the high
pay. The look and feel of
outpost Con-Am 27 has a
realism, and a level of
dehumanisation in favour of
utilitarianism (the workers'
quarters), and the grunge, and
the ordinary. The computer
technology is good for the
time period. I am certain
that the film today would be
condemned for it's lack of
modern sensibilities and any
re-make would have to socially
engineer the casting (even
though, in 2024 in similar
fields, such as oil rig
roughnecks and miners, the
majority of the workers are
male and of European-descent).

The mystery part... This is
not being done by Con-
Amalgamated, the company, at
the level of senior
management, but by the Con-Am
27 local General Manager, Mark
Sheppard. Sheppard is using
an abandoned military drug
that greatly increases worker
productivity, but after ten
months of prolonged use,
causes the worker to become
psychotic. These psychotic
episodes are resulting in
worker deaths (one wonders
what happens with the workers
who used it less and go home
to Earth after their contract
is up). O'Neil discovers that
Sheppard is smuggling this
drug into the outpost and is
encouraging the workers to use
the drug. O'Neil is going to
"clean up" Con-Am 27 and that
places him in conflict with
Sheppard. And thus you have a
western/action film in space.

The film is enjoyable for what
it is. And I still like it,
as that: a science fiction
western/thriller. Some of the
science is bad (such as the
explosive decompression) but
otherwise, it is okay for the
time period the film was made
in.

I give this film an 8 out of
10.

Some Shit Read

I recall three books I read in
1981 that had an impact on me.
These three both re-introduced
me to the author Michael
Moorcock as an adult. I had
read "Behold the Man" back in
the 1970s. I had not read any
other Moorcock at the time as
he was best known for his
Elric novels and I have never
been a big reader of sword and
sorcery fantasy (I am not big
on fantasy period and when I
do read fantasy, I prefer the
sub-genre of urban fantasy; I
will watch fantasy movies and
series though -- even sword
and sorcery...).

So, Moorcock was not a big
draw for me. I read some of
the Jerry Cornelius novels and
short fiction. It was
interesting, but not enough to
make me a fan of this series
(though, over the decades it
has grown on me). Someone, I
cannot recall who, loaned me
their copy of "The Steel Tsar"
by Moorcock. I was told that
it was fantastic. And so I
read it.

But, with trepidation initally. This novel appeared to be a pure adventure story. These are fun and light reading, but I had moved away from such as a general fare. I also preferred my adventure science fiction to be space opera.

However, I was drawn in by the introduction by Una Persson, my favourite character from the Jerry Cornelius works. And so I read the novel. In brief, it is a pretty standard Moorcock adventure. His themes are present; the multiverse, The Eternal Champion, the battle between Law and Chaos (though I prefer the Balance), and so on. He gets in his digs at colonialism, American fundamentalist Christianity, imperialism, and racism. While promoting the ideals of socialism and anarchism and portraits of alternate Nestor Makhnos.

I enjoyed the novel enough to visit the used book store and purchase the two previous novels in the trilogy, "Warlord of the Air" and "The Land Leviathan". While it is best to read the novels in order, each is a stand alone (as each takes place in a different alternate universe) so they can be read out of order and still enjoyed.

An aside from 2024: Moorcock writes proto-steampunk before the term cyberpunk was coined and before steampunk was a sub-sub genere...

The next novel is also by Moorcock but very different: it is titled "Byzantium Endures".

This book also has a strong connexion to the Jerry Cornelius series, in that the protagonist is none other than Colonel Pyat and Mrs. Cornelius is reoccuring character. That said, there is little of the fantastic in this novel (other than Pyat's preception of himself and of reality). This IS mainstream historical fiction and extremely well written. It is a character study of Maxim Arturovitch Pyatnitski, a self promoting, egotistical, ethnocentric and racist (and an anti-Semite, even though he himself is Jewish) person. In addition, he is a cocaine addict and a paeodphile (or clinically a hebephile) and really a swine of an individual. He is quick to betray, quick to switch sides (to the one that he believes will win -- he is not always correct) and is the archetype of the unreliable narrator. There are allusions to Moorcock's multiverse, but overall this is historical fiction with a great attention to detail. An example of Moorcock at his most literary.

While this is an excellent novel, spending just over 400 pages within the mind of Pyat is a drain on one's soul...

Aside from 2024: I am currently wading through the entire Pyat Quartet. I am currently taking a break before I continue the long journey through the second half of the third novel "Jerusalem Commands".

The final novel is the one that has had the most lasting impact upon me. That novel is "The War Hound and the World's Pain". This is a historical fantasy set during the Thirty Years' War during the Wars of Reformation in Europe. The protagonist is Ulrich von Bek;

von Bek is a freethinker, a mercenary who has been a soldier for both the Reformation and Counter-Reformation forces, who is jaded and no longer believes in either side, and doubts the existence of God. And thus, he finds himself lost in a forest wherein he finds a castle. The castle belongs to Lucifer who informs von Bek that He already has his soul and offers him a chance to win it back. Lucifer wants to make peace with God and has been told that He must obtain the "cure for the world's pain" (aka the Holy Grail) and von Bek is charged by Lucifer to find it. Von Bek is provided with certain metaphysical tools to aid him in this quest. In addition, Lucifer sweetens the deal by offering that He will release the soul His servant Sabrina (whom von Bek has a romantic interest in) if, and only if, he is successful in this task.

Thus it is that von Bek embarks on a series of adventures through both metaphysical realms and the ordinary real world of 17th century. He is successful in his quest. Lucifer has a meeting with God and God charges Him with the task of

redeaming Humankind, and has
full authority to dispense
knowledge at will. Lucifer
and God have agreed to have
the metaphysical realms
retreat further from the real
world; there will be no
further interference in
Humanity's progress, or lack
thereof. Lucifer decides to
make Humankind earn the
knowledge that He can now
provide freely to them.
Lucifer releases the souls of
von Bek and Sabrina, and they
leave the castle and Lucifer's
realm.

I like this novel and the
fantasy "To Reign in Hell" (by
Steven Brust) as both provide
more rationale for the
Christian mythos. The
standard mythos, as presented
from the pulpit (as opposed to
the seminary), is too "white
hats vs black hats" comic book
for me.

Aside from 2024: I explore
these themes in my novella
"Empathy for the Devil" that
has yet to find a home...

ENDNOTE

And thus ends this attempt at
re-creating SWILL #6 from
1981. As I state at the
beginning, I have less to go
on than I did for the
reconstruction of Daughter of
Swill, Mother of Scum: third
trimester. This is merely a
re-creation based on minimal
recall and that recall blurred
by four decades.

Hope that you enjoyed it...

And if you didn't, kindly fuck
off.

*** END ***

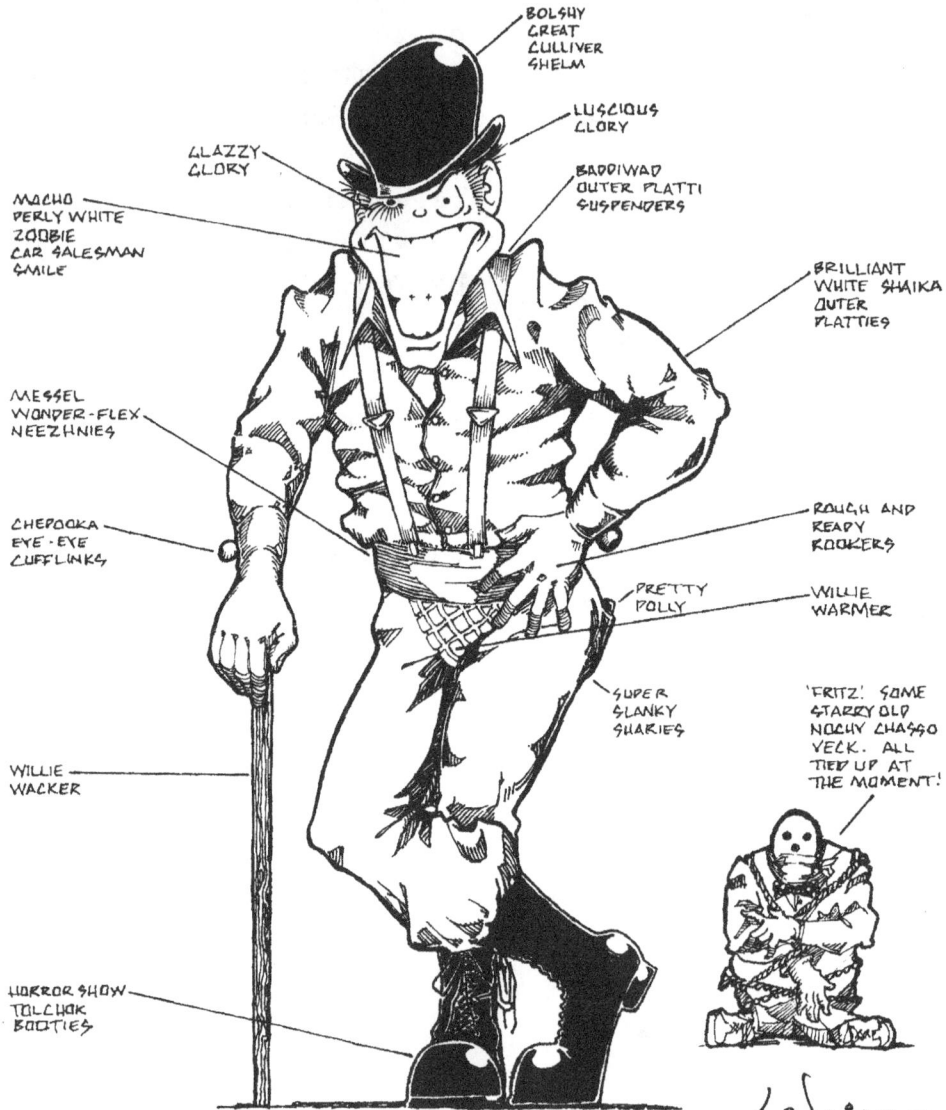

NOW THE QUESTION NEED NEVER BE RAISED AGAIN...
'WHAT THE HECK'S A DROOG?'

BOLSHY GREAT GULLIVER SHELM

LUSCIOUS GLORY

GLAZZY GLORY

BADDIWAD OUTER PLATTI SUSPENDERS

MACHO PERLY WHITE ZOOBIE CAR SALESMAN SMILE

BRILLIANT WHITE SHAIKA OUTER PLATTIES

MESSEL WONDER-FLEX NEEZHNIES

CHEPOOKA EYE-EYE CUFFLINKS

ROUGH AND READY ROOKERS

PRETTY POLLY

WILLIE WARMER

SUPER SLANKY SHARIES

'FRITZ'. SOME STARRY OLD NOCHY CHASSO VECK. ALL TIED UP AT THE MOMENT!

WILLIE WACKER

HORROR SHOW TOLCHOK BOOTIES

Kevin Davies ©1980

SWILL #6.5a

Spring 1985

Daughter of Swill, Mother of Cum.

DAUGHTER OF SWILL,
MOTHER OF SCUM
#206-3570 E. HASTINGS
VANCOUVER, B.C., V5K 2A'Z

VILE FEN | TAKE 2

Clear the set! Get those bum-fucking trekies
out of here! Get a follow spot on the subject, lighting.
Dim the gels on the backdrop. Sound cue. Check.
Camera One, ready? Check. Yeah, yeah; when the red light
goes on start talking. Right. QUIET ON THE SET!
Go sound. Start filming.
(SOUND: An alley. BUS drives past on WET PAVEMENT.
FOOTSTEPS APPROACHING from a DISTANCE. Person is wearing
COMBAT BOOTS. GARBAGE CAN is KICKED OVER. FOOTSTEPS
CONTINUE TO APPROACH. CAT GROWLS and SCAMPERS OFF
THROUGH GARBAGE STREWN ALLEY. FOOTSTEPS STOP. A CIGARETTE
is LIT. Person TAKES a DRAG from cigarette.)
NARATOR: Four years ago, in late 1980, a spontaneous
psuedo-collective known as the Vile Fen was formed.
A couple of months later, a dirty, little crudzine, called
SWILL descended upon the inocent(well, not really),
unexpecting minds of Toronto Fandom. A zine that was
to scandalise the majority of the Shit-for-Brains fan
community. SWILL pulled no punches, went straight for
the jugular of all things held near and dear, and sacred,
by fandom. It attacked fandom. It attacked science fiction.
It attacked elitism. It attacked fuzzy-headed wishful
thinking. It did so in a manner that was most crude,
such as: "Let the bastard fucking toad-spawn screw themselves
in the ass..." Well, you get the idea.
(SOUND: NARATOR takes a DRAG of CIGARETTE. THREE BEAT
PAUSE, then EXHALES.)
NARATOR: Of course, nothing has changed since that time.
In fact, it has gotten even worse than it was in 1980.
The assholes still rule. Mediafen have gained more control
over the market. Hordes of space fascists have multiplied
to goose-step across the galaxies and the far reaches of
time. And good writing continues to be smothered ever
more by the purile vomit of slothbrained hacks. The
great coils of Commercial Entertainment and Tripe, LTD.,
have increased their stranglehold upon the field.
Yeah, any change there has been, has been, for the most
part, for the worse. Though, this may just be a reflection
of society at large, for which the same is true. A society
that cries for more sensations and whom is afraid of
substance. No uneasy questions please, just give us
another helping of mindless pleasure. Everything is wonderful,
all is fine, it'll all work out; and the bombs drop in
30 minutes. As fandom is but a sub-culture of North American
Middle- Class society, one could hardly expect it not to
share similar views to that society wherin its roots lie.
And the same goes for the genre; if the consumer wants
tripe, tripe he will get, because he has proved that tripe
sells. Well baby, you better buckle up, cuz their ain't
any tripe here, I'm gonna make you think and you're in for
a rough ride.

GHETTO OFFENDER

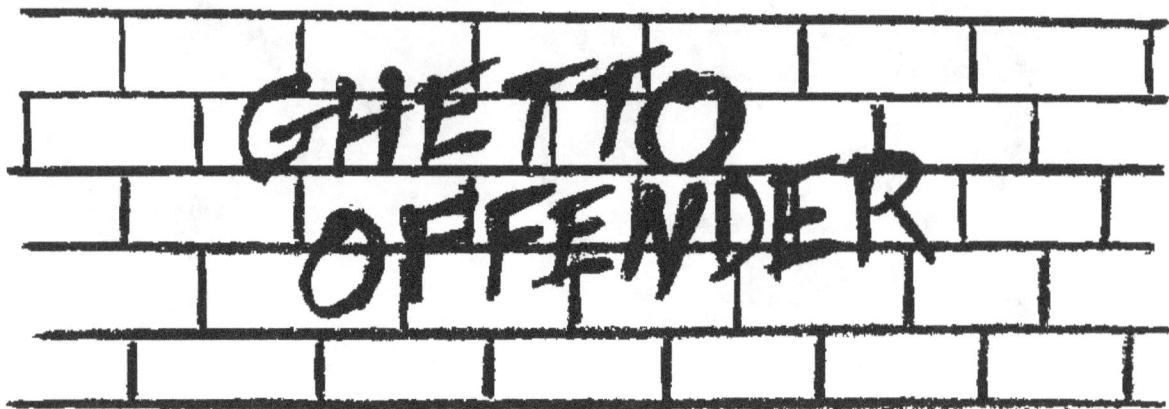

1 ESTABLISHING SHOT: EXT. - NIGHT - THE GHETTO
This is an EXTREME LONG SHOT of the ghetto wall and the
intersection of Gernsback Avenue and Campbell Boulevard.
The intersection is centre screen and in the distance.
Gernsback Avenue runs parallel to the wall, Campbell
Boulevard dead-ends at the wall. At the intersection,
there is a street lamp on the wall side of the street.
Its light reveals a figure leaning against the wall.
We CUT TO--

2 CLOSE SHOT: NARATOR
The NARATOR is a man in his late twenties with short,
dark hair and a beard and moustache. He is wearing a
black leather jacket and also wears glasses. The NARATOR
takes a drag of his cigarette and tosses it into the street.
And--

                    NARATOR
          (Bass voice.)
          Welcome to the Ghetto. I'm sure you're
          all familiar with it, you live here.
          That's right, this is the place wherein
          science fiction and its aficionados
          dwell. You probably don't recognise
          it in this guise, however. You see
          it being a wonderful, brightly lit
          cityscape, with great, glass towers
          and aircars flitting to and fro.
          The wall, if you see it in your vision
          of reality, is not of old, graffiti
          covered, red brickwork, but of crystal
          clear lucite. I'm about to give you
          a tour, a tour of the regions of the
          Ghetto which you don't see, or at
          least don't admit to. Regions that
          are as equally real as your own worldview
          of science fiction and fandom, maybe
          even more so.
          I could do with a beer about now, you
          look like you could do the same.
          Follow me, I know a great place, no
          extra charge.

3 LONG SHOT: EXT. - ALLEY & NARATOR
The alley is your typical backstreet alley. The NARATOR
stands by a wooden door, the doorstep lit by a light
above the door. The NARATOR points to the door and--

3   CONTINUED:

                    NARATOR
          This is the Starlight Hotel; there's
          a convention going on here. There's
          always a convention going on at the
          Starlight. Let's go in by the service
          entrance so that we can use the
          service elevator. The regular elevators
          are, of course, clogged with fans.

Enters through door and we CUT TO--

4   TRAVELLING SHOT: INT. - HOTEL HALLWAY
     This is a MEDIUM SHOT. We follow the NARATOR down the hall
     to the elevator. He pushes the UP button and waits.

                    NARATOR
          We're going up to what is the Hospitality
          Suite to view science fiction fans in
          one of their most natural of habitats.
          It is here at science fiction conventions
          that the inherant best and worst of
          fans makes itself apparent. Here we
          can view true testements to individuality
          as well as view one of the most bizzare
          collections of kooks and assholes ever
          assembled. Ah, here's the car.

The elevator doors open and we follow the NARATOR into the
car and we CUT TO

5   MEDIUM SHOT: INT. - NARATOR & ELEVATOR CAR INTERIOR
     The NARATOR pushes a button for one of the upper floors
     in the hotel. The car doors close and the elevator
     begins to move.

                    NARATOR
          You've been to conventions before you
          say. I'm sure you have. You know
          exactly what you're going to see and
          right you are. But, there are things
          that you shall also see that you may
          not have expected.

6   MEDIUM SHOT: INT. - ELEVATOR CAR DOORS
     The doors OPEN to reveal a hallway. We TRAVEL OUT into
     the hallway in the NARATOR'S POV. DOWN the hallway to a
     door. OPEN the door and continue to TRAVEL OUT into another
     hallway. This hallway is your regular hallway from any
     hotel. Carpeted,with wallpaper typical to hotels. There
     are fans milling about in the hallway. The NARATOR begins
     to give a running commentary on the fans we encounter as
     we continue to TRAVEL along the hall, FOCUSING on those
     fans which the NARATOR draws to our attention.

                    NARATOR
          And this is the Hospitality Suite floor.

6   CONTINUED

                        NARATOR(cont'd)
              You can tell this by the sheer number
              of fans congregated here. We seem to
              have our usual compliment of Trekies and
              Star Wars freaks all dolled up in their
              convention best. Ah yes, and there we
              have one of the countless 100 kilogram
              barbarian princesses trying her best to
              look alluring. She'd have a better
              chance at that if she were wearing more
              clothes. And there is one of terminally
              pubescent males, whose numbers are
              legion, attempting to talk up one of
              the few attractive women present.
              Ah, and there's another attractive
              woman. Oops, she's regaling her
              potential suitors with the tales of
              her past life as a Celtic lady. Nice
              bod, mind of mush though. And there's
              some guy decked out in military attire
              at the bar, probably a libertarian
              gun nut. Oh, and what do we have here?
              A bunch of people sitting on the floor
              discussing Jungian psychology. They
              look like a bunch of university students
              who were teleported here from the campus
              cafeteria. A fragment of normalacy amidst
              the freak show. There some fat, pimple
              faced kid stealing puns from Spider
              Robinson. Oh no, he's started on his
              own material, let's get clear. A couple
              of punk rockers, more mundania from the
              real world. A drunken writer surrounded
              by fans who gush at his every word.
              There's a couple getting into some heavy
              petting on the couch, while other fans
              discuss their performance with malice
              minds.
              In other words, the same old shit.
              You see it at every convention, right?
              Well, have you seen this?

       We have a MEDIUM SHOT of the Hospitality Suite and its
       occupants which we DISOLVE TO--

6A MEDIUM SHOT: INT. - HOSPITALITY SUITE
       This is still from the NARATOR'S POV. Nothing in the room
       has changed except that the people in the room are now wearing
       NAZI UNIFORMS.

                        NARATOR
              Yes, that's more true to the spirit.
              Elitists all. The cream of humanity.
              Look upon the self appointed master race.
              Down in their hearts the vast majority of

6A CONTINUED

> NARATOR(cont'd)
> science fiction fans do believe that
> they are a cut above the rest of
> humankind, whom they term, "mundanes".
> True, they are for the most part
> literate which does put them above
> the large illiterate and functual
> illiterate population, but science
> fiction fans are not the only ones
> who read. And science fiction, the
> bulk of it, is no better than the
> mainstream bestsellers and romance
> novels that science fiction fans
> revile. Although there is some scant
> basis for this elitism, it is blown
> all out of proportion by the fans
> themselves and its very roots in
> fact lies within the pages of the
> tomes so cherished by them.
> Perhaps we should look at the literature
> itself.
> Comeon, let's blow this scene.

And we CUT TO--

7   LONG SHOT: INT. - LIBRARY & NARATOR
The library is furnished in the style best described as mid-sixties
Institutional. Grey, metal bookcases, tables with formica tops
and tubular metal legs, and chairs with bright coloured, plastic
seats mounted upon tubular metal legs. The NARATOR is leaning
against a bookcase that runs along a wall towards the camera.
He approaches us, pulling books off the shelves at random.

> NARATOR
> Here we are at the Ghetto Archives.
> Let's just grab some books off the
> shelves here for a random sample of
> the genre. One, Two, Three, Four,
> Five, that ought to be enough. No?
> Okay, I'll grab two more. Seven.
> Now, why don't we sit down and examine
> these books, eh?

NARATOR sits down at one of the tables and we CUT TO--

8   CLOSE SHOT: INT. - NARATOR AT TABLE
The NARATOR spreads out the books in front of him and begins
to read off the titles.

> NARATOR
> Well, here we have, Ability Quotient
> by Mack Reynolds, Eyas by Crawford
> Kilian, Grimm's World by Vernor Vinge,
> The Inferno by Fred & Geoffrey Hoyle,
> The Iron Dream by Norman Spinrad,
> Pandora's Planet by Christopher Anvil,

8 CONTINUED

> NARATOR(cont'd)
> and Merchanter's Luck by C. J. Cherryh.
> Of that short list only the Spinrad
> book is a fluke, the novel being devoted
> to the subject of elitism in the genre,
> so let us scratch that one from the
> list. So we have six books. Pandora's
> Planet: Technologically superior aliens
> conquer Earth and open the stars for
> humankind, only to discover that they
> may have more than they bargined for
> as the humans are smarter than they are.
> The Inferno: A supernova discovered
> to actually be a quasar brings catastrophy
> to the Earth. Cameron, a particle
> physicist who was there when the object
> was discovered, through foresight is
> able to ensure survival for his region
> of the Scottish highlands and set
> himself up as a fuedal lord.
> Merchanter's Luck: A retelling in the
> science fiction motiff of the old tale
> of a noble who has lost face and name,
> reduced to common theivery, who with
> the aid of a noble lady is able to
> regain his name and rightfull station.
> Eyas, Grimm's World, and Ability Quotient
> all concern supermen, the creation of
> and/or exploits of. Nevertheless,
> the tone of elitism runs through all
> six books, whether it be elitism via
> superior intellect, wealth, rank, or
> biology. This is a major theme that
> runs through science fiction as a
> whole. Only in Eyas and The Inferno
> do we see a great deal of ordinary
> people.
> But which came first, the elitism in
> the fiction or the elitism in fandom?
> I don't know. It is certain that both
> feed off the other in the present state
> of affairs in the genre.

NARATOR stands up and walks away from the table. We FOLLOW
him as he wanders to the centre of the Library.

> NARATOR
> Again, the major quality in science
> fiction that separates it most from
> the mainstream is the abysmal lack
> of real people within its pages.
> There are myriads of superhumans,
> generals, rich merchants, political
> leaders, and great intellects, i.e.,
> the important people, but very few
> real people. What about the people

8 CONTINUED

NARATOR(cont'd)
who don't go out and save the universe?
What about the Lunar miner, the Martain
accountant, the person who pilots a
starship on a routine run between Sol
and Tau Ceti, the spaceport hooker?
These people simply don't exist in
science fiction, except as walk-ons.
Certainly they have a worthwhile story
to tell, true, they aren't going to
save all humankind, but as human beings
they obviously have something to tell
us. And yet, they remain invisible
and their absence is indeed noted
by those who live outside of the Ghetto.
And, as long as these people continue
to be absent in science fiction,
science fiction will continue to be
genre fiction, no better than spy
novels and romance stories. In other
words, junk. Oh, science fiction may
have more potential than these other
genres, but if it fails to live up to
that potential then it is no better
than those genres, perhaps even worse
as it does have the ability to go
beyond them if it would only grasp
the opportunity.
Unfortunately, with the exception of
a few authors, no real movement has
been made in this direction. There
was Timescape Books for a while
until Pocket discovered that trash
sells more and dropped the quality
line. And now, there is the New
Ace Science Fiction Specials; but
in the present market, how long will
they last? Like television, the
publishers know the same thing that
the producers long have known, you
can market trash and the consumer will
eat it up even more readily than he
will quality material. So, as trash
sells more and can be produced cheaper
than quality can, go for trash, it's
more profitable. And that's the way
that it is.
Anyhow, shall we leave the Archives?
Seen enough, eh?

And we CUT TO--

9 CLOSE SHOT: EXT. - NARATOR & WALL
This is the same as SHOT 2. The NARATOR is standing in
front of the wall. He lights a cigarette and takes a drag.
There is a THREE BEAT PAUSE and then he exhales.

9 CONTINUED

NARATOR
And here we are, back at the wall.
I've decided to cut the tour short.
Sorry about that. I'm afraid you'll
have to miss the Hack Mill, the false
glitter of the Street of Corrupted Dreams,
the Slums of the Broken Dreams, and the
place where there was once forest where
now lies a great decomposing heap of
mouldy fanzines and hack novels, wherein
rats build their nests. You're going
to have to miss all these sights,
unless you go and seek them out for
yourself. Most of you won't I'm
certain. None of you look all too
well after the few sights you have
seen. Tough.
As for myself, I shan't be giving any
further tours in the future. In fact,
I shan't be around. I'm getting out
of here. Anyone interested in joining
me? I thought not. Well, why don't
you all run along back to the Starlight.
The convention, as always, is in progress.
Me, I'm going.
Ta, ta.

We CUT TO--

10 CLOSE UP: EXT. - PICKAXE
NARATOR'S hands reach INTO the screen and pick up the pickaxe
and we CUT TO--

11 MEDIUM SHOT: EXT. - NARATOR & WALL
NARATOR swings axe at the wall and we CUT TO--

12 CLOSE SHOT: EXT. - WALL & PICKAXE
The PICKAXE bites into the brick, chipping out a hole five
centimetres in diameter and we CUT TO--

13 EXTREME LONG SHOT: EXT. - THE GHETTO
Same as SHOT 1. From this distance we see the figure of
the NARATOR swinging the pick against the wall in steady
motion. The sound of his work reaches us out of synch with
his motions.(Speed of light greater than speed of sound.)
We HOLD on this scene for TEN BEATS then FADE TO BLACK
and END.

CUT! ALL RIGHT, IT'S A WRAP! EVERYONE CAN TAKE OFF.
I want everyone back on the set by SEVEN AM TOMORROW for the
first scene of Slime Monsters from Alpha Four. Okay, go.

VILE FEN PRESS © 1984

IN CASE YOU ARE WONDERING--
YOU RECEIVED THIS BECAUSE:

___ You're a bum-fucking Trekie.
___ Trade(I give you this, you give me $10,000.)
___ LoC(you sent me a letterbomb.)
___ You contributed to SWILL.
___ You're a member of the Vile Fen.
___ You fuck sheep.
___ You're a jerk who will get pissed off and never
          speak to me again after reading this.
___ You're a piece of shit.
___ No reason whatsoever.

DAUGHTER OF SWILL,
MOTHER OF SCUM
c/o The Vile Fen
#206-3570 E. Hastings,
Vancouver, B.C.,
CANADA, V5K 2A7.

SWILL #6.5b

June 1985

DAUGHTER
of
SWILL MOTHER
of
SCUM

second trimester

IN

No Survivors

1 BLACK SCREEN. SILENCE for 3 SECONDS, THEN RUN MUSIC.
   The History of the World, Part 1 by The Damned.
                    I just hit the ground
                    Boy, have I arrived.
                    Tell the dinosaurs
                    They just won't survive--

2 .TITLE APPEARS. Daughter of Swill, Mother of Scum. PALE BLUE
   LETTERS, CENTRE SCREEN.

3 SECOND TITLE APPEARS. UNDER AND TO THE RIGHT OF FIRST TITLE.
   PALE GREEN LOWER CASE LETTERS WHICH READ, second trimester.
   HOLD FOR 20 SECONDS THEN FADE BOTH TITLES.

4. THIRD TITLE APPEARS. WHITE LETTERS, SMALL CAPS. READS:
   In The Vile Fen Press Film. HOLD FOR 10 SECONDS THEN FADE.

5. FOURTH TITLE APPEARS. RED SPRAY PAINT LETTERS WHICH READ,
   No Survivors. HOLD FOR 15 SECONDS, THEN FADE DOWN MUSIC AS WE
   DISOLVE TO--

6. ESTABLISHING SHOT: EXT. -DAY- HEAVY OVERCAST -A DESOLATE PLAIN-
   The plain is barren. A few scraggly shrubs grow here and there
   amidst patches of prairie grass. There is a dust in the air,
   a fine, white, powdery dust that is lifted from the ground by
   the wind. Off in the distance, at the far right of the screen,
   the clouds are gathered dark and black. Strange lightning plays
   between these clouds and the ground. Strange in that it appears
   slightly too orderly to be natural. No thunder accompanies the
   lightning. We hear the SOUND of an internal combustion engine
   APPROACHING from BEHIND US, and we CUT TO--

7 LONG SHOT: EXT. -CAMERA ANGLE ROTATED 90 DEGREES TO THE RIGHT
   FROM PREVIOUS SHOT A dune buggy driven by a person in a white
   radiation suit, complete with booties, gloves, hood, and mask,
   pulls to a stop in FRONT OF us, kicking up some dust. We CUT·TO--

8 CLOSE SHOT: EXT. -DRIVER OF DUNE BUGGY
   The DRIVER, who from now on will be referred to as the NARATOR
   waves to us and--
                         NARATOR
                    (Bass voice)
                    Hi there. Didn't expect to see me again on this
                    side of the Ghetto wall, did you? Well, I'm out
                    here doing some soul-searching of my own.
                    I didn't expect to meet anyone else out here,
                    though. What's that? You got lost. That explains
                    it. This is the Nuclear Plain. This is where
                    all the after-the-bomb stories in science fiction
                    take place. That? No, that's not lightning,
                    those are energy beam weapons. ·The War Zone is
                    over there. That's where Pournelle and his clones
                    play their reptile brain fantasies. No, I'm not
                    heading that way. Going for a drive in Nuke Country.
                    Want to join me? Okay, hop in.
   And we CUT TO--

9   TRAVELLING SHOT: INT.? -PASSENGER'S POV THROUGH WINDSCREEN
    The windscreen is dirty, but one can still see out of it.
    There are the background sounds of the engine, the pitch changing
    as the NARATOR shifts gears. The NARATOR is just visible in
    the driver's seat at the FAR LEFT of the FRAME. And--
                        NARATOR
            Never been out here? Not many people come out
            here these days. A few do, but mostly for
            reassurance. You know, they like to be told that
            there is a chance for survival after a full scale
            nuclear war. That America will still be around
            in some way, shape, or form after the war. You
            believe that there will be some survivors? Really?
            Ah, your a survivalist. Have a cabin in the
            mountains all stocked up with canned food and guns,
            eh? Well, I don't know. You'll certainly make
            it through the first few months, if you happen to
            be there before the bombs drop, that is. Oh, you
            have enough food to last you a year. Good idea,
            with nuclear winter-- Nuclear winter is a communist
            plot? Perpetrated by fuzzy-headed liberals.
            You know, that's strange, bub. I guess you haven't
            heard that the Pentagon has released a paper
            that says that nuke winter is a valid theory.
            Still, you may be right, those commies are lurking
            everywhere, ain't they. Ah, here we are, our
            first stop.
    The car slows to a stop. The NARATOR cuts the engine and we CUT TC

10 LONG SHOT: EXT.
    NARATOR gets out of the car and walks to the top of a hill and
    we CUT TO--

11 EXTREME LONG SHOT: EXT.
    We get a panaramic view of the valley below. A river cuts through
    the valley. On either side of its banks grow carpets of green.
    Amongst the green are villiages and a town.
                        NARATOR
            This is your typical after-the-bomb community as
            depicted in science fiction circa 1965. The
            survivors are doing all right. Civil Defence
            acted quickly after the initial attack. Survivors
            were relocated to safe areas as quickly as was
            possible, given the tools and resources needed
            to reconstruct, and all the aid that the government
            could give. The first five years were bad, the
            communities were harrassed by marauders until
            the government had restored order sufficiantly
            to wipe out these undesirables. Yes, that's right,
            the marauder bands were composed of mostly black
            and hispanic people, in other words, the poor.
            Shiftless welfare bums? Yeah, that was the
            government's opinion of them too. President?
            There is no President, the federal government is
            run by the military, though democracy has been
            allowed to return at the local level recently.

11 CONTINUED

                    NARATOR(Cont'd.)
          All in all, there are about a thousand of these
          pockets of survivors throughout America. They've
          restored the agricultural base and are managing
          okay. What? You want to go down there? Suit
          yourself, bub, but you go alone. Look, I don't
          know about you, but I have now desire to wear a
          hemp necktie. Yeah, that's right, they don't
          like strangers. Government troops, yes, but
          ordinary Joes like you and me, they lynch. Let's
          get out of here.
     CUT TO--

12 LONG SHOT: EXT. -SAME AS SHOT 10
     NARATOR walks back to the car and gets in. He starts the engine
     and we CUT TO--

13 TRAVELLING SHOT: INT. -SAME AS SHOT 9
     The NARATOR is flooring the engine. The car bounces as it zips
     over some rough terrain.
                    NARATOR
          That was your base-line science fiction after-the-
          bomb community. Some are rosier, some are worse,
          in all a sizable segment of the American population
          survive. I want to skirt the real bad areas, the
          ones similar to the vision put forth in The Road
          Warrior and A Boy and His Dog. I like living and
          plan to continue to do so. Where are we going?
          Nowhere in paticular. As I said when I first
          picked you up, I'm out here for myself. Just want
          to drink in all this desolation for my own reasons
          which are none of your business. Got that.
          Yeah, yeah, I'll try and show you a survivalist
          hole afore I bug out. Yeah, hole. What else
          would you call it? A shelter. Well, a rat's
          hole is also a shelter, so why try and pretty it
          up? Call it what it is, a hole. Yeah, I am.
          You've heard the cliche about rats deserting a
          sinking ship, eh? Well, I see the analogy as
          being correct. Hey bub, if you don't like what
          I say you can always leave. I don't really need
          your company. All of you survivalists are just
          acting like a pack of rats, running off to your
          holes with you hoard of food, weapons, and gold
          to hide until it's safe to come out. What's so
          macho and manly about that? You don't try and
          do anything to halt the escalation of the arms
          race, do you. In fact, your the lot which think
          that Ronald Reagan is too liberal. Oh, I see,
          it's not only nuclear war you fear. Economic
          collapse? All them blacks are going come for
          your precious possessions, rape your wife and
          daughter, and kill you. Tell me, have you always
          had this paranoia about blacks? I see. What's that?
          Nuclear war won't happen anyway. Then why are you

13 CONTINUED

> NARATOR(Cont'd)
>
> spending all that money on a rat hole in the
> mountains? Just in case. Ah, I see. Just in
> case the liberals trash Reagan's Star Wars
> programme. I hate to tell you this, bub, but
> it don't matter one damn what the liberals in
> your country do, 'cause Star Wars just ain't
> going to work. How do I know? Simple. Star
> Wars is designed to provide a defence system that
> would knock out all the Soviet missiles before
> they reached American targets, thus sparing
> America from a Soviet attack. Right? Okay,
> One: such a system based in space is going to
> be so complex and costly, but mostly complex,
> and the greater the complexity of a weapons
> system, the greater the chance of there being
> a fuck up, ie. something not working when you
> need it to. TWO: such a system is going to be
> extremely vulnerable. It's damned easy to destroy
> and even easier to disable. Input this, all the
> Soviets need to do is send up a space mine near
> an American battle station, a space mine equiped
> with a thermonuclear device. Explode that once
> the attack is started and even if the bomb doesn't
> damage the station, the electro-magnetic pulse
> will knock out all its electronics, rendering it
> useless. And there are many other ways of knocking
> out one of these battle stations. THREE: there is
> no way of making such a system even 80% effective
> let alone the 95% that's being bantered about.
> The Soviets can just build a lot more missiles
> and overwhelm the system. The Soviets will have
> submarine launched cruise missiles soon which won't
> travel outside of the Earth's atmosphere to reach
> target, so how are you going to get 'em. And even
> if the American's do develop that satellite that
> can spot and track subs, you can always sink a
> platform of missiles down deeper; missiles which
> when given the launch signal are released, float
> to the surface, launch, and cruise under radar to
> their targets. Sorry, bub, but Star Wars ain't
> going to provide you any safe shield to cower
> under. Eh? Well, that's right, you do still
> have your rat hole in the mountains. You wanted
> to see a survivalist hole, didn't you? Well,
> here we are.

The car stops and the NARATOR gets out. We CUT TO--

14 LONG SHOT: EXT. -SURVIVALIST HOLE
It's a concrete bunker-type structure built into the side of
a hill. It possesses a very thick steel door at its entrance.
The door is open. The trees surrounding the shelter are all
dead. There are some grasses growing in the area and a few
sickly bushes. The NARATOR walks up to the entrance.
> NARATOR

14 CONTINUED

NARATOR
This one's been abandoned for about a month.
What? It looks like yours? A coincidence.
Probably had it built by the same company.
Want to see a survivalist? He's over here.
I'm suprised the others didn't find him before
they left. This way.

We FOLLOW the NARATOR into the forest of dead trees for a distance
of about 300 metres.

NARATOR
There's not much left of him, I'm afraid.
These are hard times and the scavengers, the few
that are left are very thorough; food is hard to
come by. What happened to him? Well, the war
occurred in March. The nuclear winter was severe.
Lasted about eight months; spring and summer never
came. Many of the plants and animals died.
The survivalists remained holed up until February,
by which time they were running out of food. The
man of the house set out with his trusty automatic
rifle to bag some meat. He ran into a wolf pack
here. Wolves generally don't mess with humans,
we tend to win such battles. But these wolves
were very, very hungry. Our survivalist, a businessm
by trade was not quite quick enough with his rifle.
He got one wolf, but the other five brought him
down. They killed and ate him. Eh? Looks like
your gun.   That's because it is your gun. That's
your corpse, fucker. We're in the real world now,
not the sci-fi world. A real world where the idiots
blew us sky high in March of '84. You and your
family were vacationing here at your rat hole when
it happened. It's now April of '85. Your dead,
so is your family. Yor wife, and two kids were
killed by a bear, 200 klicks from here last week.
They were the last ones, I think. In North America,
Europe, Japan, Coastal and Northern China, and the
Soviet Union, there is almost no one left. And
whatever few survivors there may be, they are all
dying of starvation, of sickness, from predators,
including each other. In five years there will be
nobody left. All dead. People are getting by
in the rest of the world, mostly in the southern
hemisphere. But they got the winter too, not as
bad, but bad enough. They were hit hard. Many of
them were killed too. Many are still dying. They
will survive, humanity will survive, but not here
it won't. In those northern regions mentioned
above, there will be, NO SURVIVORS!
You're crying. Hey don't fall apart on me. You
are still alive, in our real world. This shit
hasn't happened here, yet. Makes you think, though,
don't it. Maybe if you sci-fi survivalist, pro-bomb
types spent as much time thinking about how to
prevent nuclear war as you do on how you're going

14 CONTINUED

SIX

NARATOR(Cont'd)
survive it, we might all be able to ensure that it never happens. And by all I don't just mean science fiction fans, but ALL of us. Honestly, it's in your own best interest. It's a question of whether you want to live or you want to die. 'Cause if it does happen, most of us are going to die, and you can forget all your wishfull fantasies about surviving to forge a new America. In North America there wil be, NO SURVIVORS.

HOLD for 10 SECONDS THEN FADE TO BLACK.
ROLL CREDITS AND END.

XXXXXXXXXXXXXXXXXXXXXXXXXXXXXXXXXXXXXXXXXXXXXXXXXXXXXXXXXXXXXXXX
MINUTES OF MARCH 1985 PRODUCTION MEETING
RE: Daughter of Swill, Mother of Scum; first trimester
STUDIO EXECUTIVE VAUGHN: Too elitist.
WRITER NEIL: Please elaberate.
VAUGHN: (no comment)
STUDIO EXECUTIVE JULIET: I find the bit about there being "few attractive women present" to be politically incorrect and sexist. You shouldn't judge people by their appearence alone.
NEIL: How one preceives what is and isn't attractive is relative. I have my own tastes and my tastes are far ranging compared to most guys. I may like big hips but--
JULIET: Well I can wag my hips for all that that's worth, however--
NEIL: Juliet, you may read science fiction, among other things, but you have yet to be to a science fiction convention. At a science fiction convention you will find the largest congregation of obese people in the world--
JULIET: You still shouldn't judge people by their appearence--
NEIL: Name me one human being who doesn't to some degree. We just all have our individual tastes and my individual tastes happen to include no woman under 20, as they either act like or are giggling bubble heads, as well my tastes also do not include 100 kilogram lardballs. And, as you are being so high and mighty why don't tell me, have you ever judged a person on personal appearence alone.
JULIET: Yes, but--
NEIL: I think you're getting your nose out of joint because I mentioned "women". Look that part over again, I don't make the guys appear very attractive either.
(PAUSE TO CONSULT SCRIPT WHICH RESOLVES ARGUEMENT FOR THE PRESENT.)
ANNONYMOUS STUDIO EXECUTIVE: You attack the elitism of fans, but fail to acknowledge that they are are a group of people who are as a whole fairly intelligent and interesting.
NEIL: I'll agree with that more or less. The problem is, that science fiction fans think that they are the only ones who possess these qualities, that they are a cut above the rest. Not so. In fact, in my work with radio I have met a far greater number of people who are interesting and intelligent than I have in fandom. As well, many people in the art and music communities also possess these qualities, but to fans, they are just dumb mundanes.
MEETING ADJOURNED TO GO TO D.O.A. CONCERT
XXXXXXXXXXXXXXXXXXXXXXXXXXXXXXXXXXXXXXXXXXXXXXXXXXXXXXXXXXXXXXXX

DAUGHTER OF SWILL, MOTHER OF SCUM
                        second trimester
In The Vile Fen Press Film

NO SURVIVORS

a Neil Williams Production

Released by Black Dwarf Productions
c 1985 Vile Fen Press

vile fen press is a subsidiary of black dwarf productions

filmed in MONOCHROME

shot on location at the Wasteland Studios in Sudbury, Ontario

DAUGHTER OF SWILL,
MOTHER OF SCUM
c/o Vile Fen Press
204-20 Goldbeck Lane,
Waterloo, Ontario,
CANADA, N2J 4L1.

SWILL #6.5c

June 1986

reconstructed version

DAUGHTER OF SWILL Mother of scuM

third trimester

Take Two: an intro

Sound cue. Check.
Camera One, ready? Check. Right. QUIET ON THE SET!
Go sound. Start filming.

(SOUND: A bare stage. FOOTSTEPS APPROACHING from a DISTANCE.
FOOTSTEPS CONTINUE TO APPROACH. FOOTSTEPS STOP.)

(LIGHTING: Single spot on the NARATOR.)

NARATOR: (He is a man in his mid-60s, about 180 cm tall, with
short hair -- once black, but now white -- who is wearing a dark
grey business casual shirt and jeans, and runners)

Hello. This is **NOT** the original issue of Daughter of SWILL,
Mother of Scum: third trimester.

There was an issue published in 1986. But, I have no copies of
that issue. And it would appear that nobody has any copies of
that issue ((The print run was small and distribution was
limited to Waterloo, Ontario and some copies handed out in
Toronto. It is possible that a copy does exist in some fanzine
archive, somewhere, though this is a remote possibility. Of
course, I would be very happy to be wrong. And have my
wrongness proven by someone sending me a scanned pdf of the
original 1986 Daughter of SWILL, Mother of Scum: third
trimester...

So, here is where we are in 2024. I have no copy of the issue
of Daughter of SWILL, Mother of Scum: third trimester. Now, I
did devote the entire issue of SWILL #35 to the same topic,
though in more depth. I considered just printing the editorial
from SWILL #35 as a sort of place-holder for Daughter of SWILL,
Mother of Scum: third trimester; then I decided no.

(He shrugs.)

Instead, I am going to attempt to re-create what I wrote back in
1986. This will not be easy. I have to remember that back then
I had begun, then abandoned a Bachelor's degree in English
Literature, worked for a few years, and had started a Bachelor's
degree in Social Anthropology. I have to control and not let
too much of my 2024 self leak in (a person holds a completed
Bachelor's degree and two post-graduate degress and over twenty
five years of teaching experience). I will try and maintain the

tone of the first two Daughter of SWILL issues. I have a vague
recollection of the general settings I used in this issue, and a
sort of memory that it was based on an article that I read on
how primary senses and environment have a great impact on an
animal's perception of reality; and that the worldview of an
alien, should be, very alien.

(NARRATOR rubs his clean shaven chin.)

Given that the whereabouts, or even the continued existence of
Daughter of SWILL, Mother of Scum: third trimester of 1986,
remains unknown. I will hand you over to an avatar of my
younger self, who will present a re-creation of this issue.

(NARRATOR pauses)

With hope, you will enjoy it...

CNALIEN ALIENS

1 ESTABLISHING SHOT: EXT. - NIGHT - THE GHETTO
This is an EXTREME LONG SHOT of the ghetto wall and the
intersection of Martian Alley and Venusian Boulevard.
Venusian Boulevard runs parallel to the frame and Martian
Alley leads to a distant spaceport where a ship is lifting
off.

There is a street lamp at the intersection. Below the street
lamp and in its pool of light, its light, a figure stands.
We CUT TO--

2 CLOSE SHOT: NARATOR
The NARATOR is a man in his late twenties with short Mohawk. He
is wearing a black leather jacket over a neon pink The Damned
t-shirt, and black jeans.

NARATOR
(Bass voice.)
Okay, we are back in the Ghetto. I am mostly me, but I am also
not.
I am a mental simulation of myself; what that means is this.
In 2024, my mature self in his sixties, will attempt to write as
me back in my twenties, as I was in 1986.

Whatever. We will see how this goes...
(he points up Martian Alley)
This is the way to the spaceport, but we are not going there
just yet.
(he snaps his fingers)
We CUT TO --

3 MEDIUM SHOT: INT. STARLIGHT HOTEL BALLROOM
A typical hotel ballroom that could seat 130 for dinner and a
small dancefloor for a wedding reception, which has been set up
with a large dancefloor and numerous small tables of six. There
is a crowd of fans, all in costume. Some are sitting, some are
milling around the bar, some are socialising, some are dancing.

NARATOR
This is the Ballroom of the Starlight Hotel. It is evening and
so the Costume Bacchanal is already in progress.

4 MEDIUM SHOT: PANNING ACROSS THE COSTUMES

NARATOR
Okay some various Star Trek outfits... There is a Klingon, an
Orion slave girl, several Mr. Spocks, a red shirt who is not
dead yet.. Over there are some Star Wars costumes. A couple of
Princess Leias, a Darth Vader, a Chewbacca, some Stormtroopers,
a Luke, and overweight Han Solo...   Some Ghostbusters. A
couple as Nostromo crew. Buck Rogers and Wilma Deering.
Assorted crew from Battlestar Galactica and a Cylon. But all
very human, or at least very humanoid. And NOT very alien.
(he snaps his fingers)
We CUT TO --

5 LONG SHOT: EXT. - NIGHT - THE SPACEPORT
This is a flat tarmaced field. In the near distance is the main
passenger spaceport terminal that is all bright and made of spun
crystal spires and lucite. Around us are the cargo terminal and
fuel depots. We are standing next to an ordinary looking
building that would be at home within any late
20th century industrial park. There is a sign that above the
entrance.
The sign shifts languages cycling to another every 15 seconds.
At this moment it flashes up in English "DRINK".

NARATOR
This is the part of the spaceport that your average SF
interstellar freighter or tramper would be directed to land at.
And this is the spaceport bar that the average SF starship
freighter captain would frequent. Shall we go in and have a
look-see?
We CUT TO --

6 MEDIUM SHOT: INT. SPACEPORT BAR
This is your typical bar that caters to a working class
clientele. It is not a "dive, but it is not "upscale"

either. It is a place to go and have some drinks, but the
possibility exists that some of the customers may engage in
a fight if a situation arose... The decor is neutral and
pragmatic. Nothing stands out, so nothing can really
offend the eyes (or other senses), and all surfaces appear
to be easy to clean. There is some low volume instrumental
music playing in the background that contains elements of
both jazz and blues, but is neither. What dominates is the
cacophony of multiple voices (and languages) all speaking at
same time and reverberating off the walls in this enclosed
space.

NARATOR
So this is a real spaceport bar, not the one for the
tourists. This is where spacers relax after a long
day of wrangling the robots to unload and load cargo.
Or after navigating the atmospheric descent and making
landfall on this planet you have never been too. Oh,
the spacers that are regular travellers to this world?
Most of them have friends, partners, family in the city;
they only come here to do business.

You can see that the clientele are more diverse that
those at the Costume Bacchanal at the Starlight...
We CUT TO --

7 MEDIUM SHOT: PANNING ACROSS THE BAR

NARATOR
So we are in the "normal area". The gravity is set
to .87 G and there is an oxygen/nitrogen atmosphere.
And most of the patrons are not very strange. There
are some lifeforms that are descended from an ancestor
that was reptile-like, others from avian-like, still
more that are amphibian-like, and various mammalian-like
forms. There is a good argument for this.
We CUT TO --

8 CLOSE SHOT: NARATOR

NARATOR
It goes like this and is based on pragmatic concepts. A
multicellular animal has to eat, digest, excrete and move.
The most basic form is a tube. There is an eating orifice
at the front, food is digested in the middle, and excreted
from the middle or near to the rear, and the rear is a
flagellum or tail that propels the creature in its

environment. Sensory apparatus would tend to evolve in
the front of the animal. Along with that would be the
central nervous system and ganglia cluster (proto-brain).
This is called bilateral symmetry.

So, if this is the norm in evolution, then most
intelligent life would tend to be "humanoid" in
appearance.
(NARATOR shrugs)
Of course, we are basing this all on a single case, Earth.
We CUT TO --

9 LONG SHOT: EXT. - NIGHT - THE SPACEPORT AND STARSHIP
A different spot on the flat tarmaced field. In the left of
the frame in the near distance we can see the Spaceport Bar,
distinguished by its lit sign cycling through different
languages. In the background of frame right is one of the
landing legs of a starship and a lowered ramp. The starship
is clean and in good repair, but it has a utilitarian feel to
it and it has experienced some wear (not shiny and brand new).

NARATOR
That means we have to get away from that single case, the Earth.
(BEAT)
Come aboard.
(NARRATOR exits up the lowered ramp)
(Off Screen)
Yes, follow me up the ramp.

10 MEDIUM SHOT: INT. STARSHIP COCKPIT
This is a cockpit more than a bridge. There are three seats,
and two more can be dropped down into place if needed.
Everything is neat and tidy, but certainly not spotless. There
is a curved widescreen display that shows the ship exterior.
NARATOR
Valeria?

VALERIA
(Female voice with slight Slavic accent)
Yes, Neil.

NARATOR
Do you have the coordinants pre-loaded?

VALERIA
Jump coordinants are loaded. It will take five Jumps to reach
our destination.

NARATOR
Sounds great, Lera. Take us up, please.

VALERIA
Acquiring course from Traffic Control.
(BEAT)
Initiating atmospheric drive. Liftoff.

On the display the spaceport slowly, then more rapidly, drops
below us.

NARATOR
Lera, how about some music.

VALERIA
Certainly, Neil.

Howling Wind by The Alarm fills the cockpit
And we CUT TO --

11: EXTREME LONG SHOT: EXT. 400 KM ABOVE AN ALIEN PLANET
The planet is Earth-like and showing near gibbous. The
vegetation is light lime-green in colour and the oceans are
periwinkle. The darkened planet shows a pattern of clustered
lights. There is a technological civilisation here.

The starship drops out of Jump above the planet.
And we CUT TO --

12: MEDIUM SHOT: INT. STARSHIP COCKPIT
Same as Shot 10. The planet is on the display.

VALERIA
Arrived.

NARATOR
Thanks, Lera. Any activity?

VALERIA
Affirmative. The locals have dispatched a ship. That ship is
on an intercept course with us.

NARATOR
Weapons?

VALERIA
The ship does possess weapons.

NARATOR
Shields up.

VALERIA
Initiated. I have been analysing the alien broadcasting
systems. It would appear that we have encountered a species
that has spherical symmetry and places little emphasis on
vision. The primary senses are auditory and magnetic fields.

NARATOR
Can you translate any of their broadcasts?

VALERIA
Negative. Eventually, yes. That will take time though.

NARATOR
How much time?

VALERIA
At least one month.

NARATOR
Yikes. Lera, can you assign a part of yourself to work that
task, low priority.

VALERIA
I will.
(BEAT)
The ship on intercept course is initiating communications.

NARATOR
Put it onscreen, please.
And we CUT TO --

13: CLOSE SHOT: INT. STARSHIP DISPLAY SCREEN
The picture on the display is distorted. It is set to the
brightness, contrast, and colour perceptions of a different
species, and one for whom the sense of sight is not a primary
sense. There is an odd, obviously patterned, but still
gibberish cacophony of audio. There is a spherical shape
centre-screen, but the image is blurred and the frame rate is
different to that used by humans.
(We take this in for several BEATS)

VALERIA
Alien ship is shifting power to their weapons. Initiating
evasive Jump.

The display screen goes blank.

VALERIA
We are one point three lightyears from the alien planet. No
pursuit by the aliens.

NARATOR
Thanks, Lera. Good work.

VALERIA
Do you still want me to work on translation of the alien
language?

NARATOR
Sure. But, leave it until we get back.

NARATOR turns to look into the Fourth Wall.

Alien, is going to be alien. Really alien. We may not even
communicate using the same senses. Our perception of light
colour, sound will be different. Our primary senses won't be
the same. They may have senses that we have no reference for.
Their environment and how they experience it may be different as
well. This will impact how they use language. We may not even
be able to communicate and may only be able to communicate in
the areas of mathematics.

The universe is going to be stranger than we think.

NARATOR turns away.

Lera, can you take us home, please.

VALERIA
Setting course. Initiating Jump.
And we CUT TO --

14: LONG SHOT: EXT. - DAY - THE SPACEPORT AND STARSHIP
Same as Shot 9, but in the daytime.

NARATOR
And so, the dilemma. What is the fine line between an alien
that is so different that you cannot understand it or its

actions are irrational and the "alien" that is just a human in
makeup? That depends on the type of story you are telling, the
conventions of the sub-genre the story fits within, and the form
the plot takes. If it is action based, then the human in makeup
may work best. If the emphasis of the story is on an idea or
concept then the more alien the alien is, the better. And if it
is a story that focuses on character, and the protagonist is an
alien, the alien has to have enough in common with humans so
that the human reader/audience can identify with the alien; so
that it can be a character and not a thing.
(BEAT)
However, at the end of the day, we are talking about fiction.
About telling a tale. Because we are writing science fiction,
we do want a degree of probability in the story.
(BEAT)
But, we are just writing fiction. And that is fine.
(BEAT)
In all likelihood, real aliens will be really, really alien.

FADE TO BLACK

END

* *

END TITLES

Empty stage. Single spot on the NARATOR. We are back in 2024
and he is again in his mid-60s and wearing the same outfit as in
Take Two.

NARATOR:
So that was based on what I recall of the content of the
original issue. There is not much more I can say about Daughter
of Swill, Mother of Scum: third trimester. With hope you
enjoyed this reconstruction. I would like to think that the
reconstruction has some accuracy, but only time will tell if
that is so ;)
(BEAT)
So this is a wrap.
Lera, please take us out.

NARATOR walks off stage and out of frame.

A blonde woman in her 20s who stands about 160 cm in height
walks into frame and on stage. She steps into the spotlight and
looks into the camera. We can see she has green eyes.

VALERIA
You have been watching a reconstruction of Daughter of Swill,
Mother of Scum: third trimester.
This was originally written and published in 1986 by Neil
Williams.
This reconstructed version was written in 2024 by Neil Williams
(BEAT)
This has been a Vile Fen Press film
Released by Black Dwarf Productions
(BEAT)
Vile Fen Press is a subsidiary of Black Dwarf Productions,
which is a subsidiary of Relling Vatch Software,
which is a subsidary of Klatha Entertainment.
all of which are imprints of Uldune Media
(BEAT)
Copyright © 1986 - 2025 Uldune Media
(BEAT)
The role of NARATOR was performed by Neil Williams
The role of VALERIA was performed by myself, Alina Kabanova
(BEAT)
Filmed in MONOCHROME
at Vacant Industrial Lot Studios in Woodstock, Ontario, Canada.
(BEAT)
Thank you for watching
Good bye / Proshchay

VALERIA smiles and bows
And we FADE TO BLACK

END

SWILL #7

February 2001

Swill

Online

Back   Next

Table of Contents

Back   Next

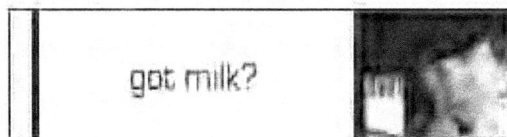

Editorial

          Next

Last year, when I first mused the notion of reviving Swill, an old droog of mine asked the question -- "Why? Just because it's the 20th anniversary, or because you want to piss off fandom?" At the time, I really didn't have a solid answer. I shrugged and replied, "Mostly, 20th anniversary." And that was that.

I've given the question some thought -- not much, but some -- since then.

Back in 1981, the primary reasons for publishing Swill were:

- because it really ticked off SF fandom in Ontario, Canada
- because it was fun
- because of the local notoriety I received

As I mulled over the re-launch of Swill in the latter months of 2000, the primary reasons for this endeavour were:

- pure nostalgia
- the hope that it would be fun
- miscellaneous reasons

In essence, the revival of Swill was to be a retrospective, an opportunity to gather in and re-connect with some of the old contributors for on final "kick-at-the-can". Nostalgia, period.

However, as the time ticks down toward launch the miscellaneous reasons began to creep forward in prominence.

A nostalgic retrospective just wouldn't be true to the spirit of Swill. In fact, it would be inappropriate to say the least. Swill was a vicious, angry, intentionally offensive, silly, irreverent, and obnoxious series of attacks on the science fiction genre and, in particular, science fiction fandom. Any revival of Swill would have to embody that same spirit...

The problem is, I have changed -- twenty years will do that. I ceased to be a science fiction fan in 1986, undergoing the quiet transformation into a reader. Of the literature that I read, a significant portion continues to be within the genre of science fiction, but I am no longer a science fiction fan.

With the exception of an 18 month period between 1992 and 1993, when I was performing participant observation research on subcultural groups -- including science fiction fandom -- that host annual public special events, I have had no connexion with science fiction fandom. As a part of my life, science fiction fandom has become, well; completely irrelevant. The concerns, ideals, mores, and virtues -- such as they are -- of this subcultural group have ceased to be mine. I have no anger directed toward science fiction fandom, only mild contempt.

A contempt that arises, as the old cliché says, out of my familiarity with the subject group rooted within experience and observation. This contempt is largely not even specific to science fiction fandom, but is shared with other hobby/leisure based subcultural groups that exhibit the same traits of useless tribalism. Still some of this contempt is specific to science fiction fandom and its ideology that the members of this subculture are somehow inherently superior to the rest of us that exist outside of it.

Nevertheless, it is a mild contempt. Mild, as it rarely crosses my mind because I don't ordinarily even think about these subcultural groups, let alone science fiction fandom specifically. Hardly the sort of feeling to use as the foundation for the re-launch of Swill.

And yet... There is something older and deeper that rises out of the backbrain. A primal and primate behaviour that possesses a certain pleasure.

There is a short sequence of film that I used to show when I taught intro Anthropology. In this clip there are two young chimps and some chickens. The first chimp would toss out some feed to the chickens. The chickens would approach the two chimps as they gobbled the feed. When the chickens got within reach, the second chimp would whack the closest chicken with a stick. In a flurry of flapping and clucking the chickens would scatter. The first chimp would toss out some more feed and the chickens -- being chickens -- would once again go after the feed and draw close to the pair of chimpanzees. I have no idea as to how long the two chimps let this loop continue nor do I confess to truly know what these chimps were thinking and feeling. I will offer the opinion that I think that they were playing a game. They were teasing the chickens.

And that is why Swill has returned. The major reason for reviving Swill is so that I can play a game, a game called teasing science fiction fandom. I think that this game will be more akin to disturbing an anthill than teasing chickens -- I'm not certain as to what would make good feed -- but I sure do intend to have some fun. With hope, some of the old contributors will decide to join in the game too.

Table of Contents   Next

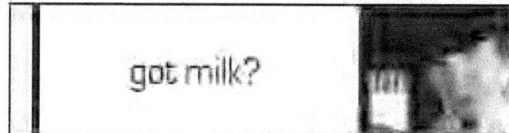

The State of the Genre: some observations

Back   Table of Contents   Next

Over the past few months, I have perused many science fiction fan sites on the internet. According to the general consensus within the subculture:

- science fiction is dead
- science fiction is dying
- science fiction has gone downhill
- science fiction is in crisis

Rubbish. Looking backward over the past score of years and comparing them to the present, the genre has never been healthier.

In reference to the first two fannish claims, I present the following observations.

Within a medium-sized Canadian city (population 300,000) that does not have a specialty store devoted to the genres of science fiction and fantasy, in most general bookshops, science fiction and fantasy command, on average, a larger proportion of shelf space than any other fiction genre. Only the romance section offers any real competition in the quest for shelf space. True, individual stores will vary, but on average, science fiction and fantasy have larger sections. This pattern is very apparent in the book superstores, such as Chapters and Indigo.

Now, it is also true that the majority of small general book retailers, such as Coles here in Canada, tend to stock their science fiction sections with a predominance of Star Trek, Star Wars, and other media related novels and novelisations along with copies of genre bestsellers. That said, these are general book retailers. I do not expect to find the re-issue of Ellison's Deathbird Stories in the science fiction section any more than I would expect to find a re-issue of Solzhenitsyn's One Day in the Life of Ivan Denisovich in the literature section at my local Coles. However, if I want a copy of either book I can order it into the store or purchase it online.

There are more science fiction books being published than ever before. In the magazine trade -- while the fates of individual science fiction and fantasy magazines ebb and flow -

- there is an increase in the number of professional science fiction and fantasy magazines published.

Media science fiction has established a definite niche for itself to the extent that science fiction has become -- just like medical, lawyer, and police shows -- a standard genre on television. Similar for film. And, like the other standard genres, one can expect that there will be at least one new television series produced and at least one new film released each year that is science fiction.

There is little observable evidence to indicate that the genre is dead or dying.

The claims that science fiction has "gone downhill" or that it is "in crisis" are highly subjective statements. Usually, these claims refer to the decline in the frequency that new material is being published within the claimant's preferred subgenre of science fiction -- be that hard science, military, science fantasy, "New Wave', or whatever. The popularity of individual subgenres fluctuates over time and the current popularity of any given subgenre is not a reflection of the health of the genre as a whole.

What these doom and gloom claims are actually in reference to is the perceived loss of science fiction as the special literature to specific group of people -- science fiction fandom. Science fiction fandom no longer owns the genre; nor has it for quite some time, but the belief that fandom owns science fiction is now much harder to maintain with any degree of rationality.

If there is any group that can be said to own the genre, it is the readers -- be they casual or steady. And most readers are not fans. And a good thing too. If the genre had to depend solely upon fandom as its audience, it would have become extinct decades ago. Fandom itself is not a large enough market to sustain the genre. Readers sustain the genre. And the overwhelming majority of science fiction readers are happily oblivious to the existence of fandom. Some have had a taste of fandom, usually through attending a local convention, and found it to be either unsatisfactory or unpalatable and therefore do not seek to repeat the experience. And others are ex-fans, such as myself.

While science fiction readers tend to be unaware or indifferent to fandom, fandom tends to harbour a strong dislike and distrust for those that are "just readers". Readers, well, aren't fannish. They don't know all the subcultural acronyms and sayings, they call the genre sci-fi, they don't know what the regional convention circuit is, they don't realise that the person they are disagreeing with about the fact that 'The Postman' was originally a piece of short fiction is the Lord High Ruler of the Video Room and a local Big Name Fan. In short, they are not fans. They are not part of the science fiction fan subculture. And, most have no interest in becoming members of that subculture. Readers are outsiders...

Or are they?

A better case could be made that science fiction fans are the outsiders, given that the readers must outnumber them by a factor of no less than ten to one.

As for the state of the genre -- From my perspective, it is healthy, strong, and fully integrated into popular culture. Things have never been better.

Back   Table of Contents   Next

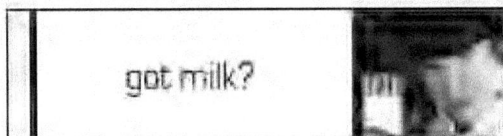

Is There Anything Unique About Fandom?

Back   Table of Contents   Next

Science fiction fandom likes to think of itself as being unique and in some manner different from the mundane mainstream of contemporary culture. But, it really isn't.

The ordinary member of society engages in work, fullfilling the basic physical needs (eating, hygine, and sleep), procurement of resources (food, drink, and cleaning and hygine products), social interaction (friends, family, co-workers, aquantainces), and the leisure activities that serve to fullfill their individual mental and/or emotional and/or spiritual and/or additional physical needs. Leisure activities may be solitary or occur within groups. When in a group activity, they may be informal (getting together with a group of friends to see a movie or to play a game of cards) or more formalised (attending a dinner party, playing the weekly curling match, participation in some form of club or organisation). Of the more formalised leisure activities that individuals participate in, some of these may occur within the context of a subcultural group -- be that religious, ethnic, political or leisure-based.

Most individuals balance their leisure activities, i.e. they have several different leisure activities that bring them into contact with different groups of individuals. Some persons, however, focus their leisure activities. One activity is given primacy over the others so that they interact with an overlapping set of groups or just a single group of individuals. This is most common in regards to leisure activites that occur within a subcultural context.

Science fiction fandom is a leisure-based subculture. Little theatre groups, internet newsgroups, amateur sport clubs, historical re-creation groups also have leisure-based subcultures. On the surface, it would appear that these leisure-based subcultures have little in common, but, if you look deeper, there is a pervasive sameness to all of these groups.

All have their own subcultural acronyms, sayings, and history -- both mythic and actual. All have their internal politics, feuds, and power struggles. All have a sense of tribalism, whether it is mild or strong. All have some individuals who make the subculture their way of life -- be that little theatre, rugby football, the Society for Creative Anachronism, or science fiction fandom -- to the exclusion of all other activities. All have individuals

8

who engage in status climbing games in pursuit of ephemeral power. Ephemeral because in the grand scheme of things outside of the subculture, the fact that you have fought your way to the top to become the Queen of props, or the Grand Poohbah of the newsgroup, or the Baron of Itsyourdelusion, or the Bonspiel Master of the Lower Lonsdale Curling Club, or the Grand Wizard of the consuite, really means very little. Maybe you can put a spin on it and work it into a resume, but that is all that it is worth in society as a whole.

So science fiction fandom is really no different from these other leisure based subcultures -- except for the ideology of superiority. Now all of these subcultures have some form of ideology of superiority, but it tends to be relative to the subculture's competitors. To rugby football fans, their team is superior (or should be) and their sport is superior to its strongest competitor -- soccer. Little theatre people view themselves as being superior to those who don't support the arts who are viewed as being competition, threat, or both. Roman re-creation groups tend to view themselves as superior to the SCA -- a competitor. Internet newsgroups members view their newsgroup of choice to be superior to similar competing newsgroups. Science fiction fandom views itself as being superior not to competitors, such as comic book fandom or Star Trek fandom (in fact, these competitors tend to be viewed as potential allies and/or poor delluded souls who are on the right path but have yet to see the light), but to everybody else. (This could be an indication of paranoia within science fiction fandom -- that everybody else is seen as being a competitor or a threat.)

And what is the basis of the superiority of science fiction fandom?
- science fiction fans are regular readers
- science fiction fans are scientific literates
- science fiction fans have a "sense of wonder"

It is indeed true that science fiction fans are regular readers. This does place them within a select group within the general population -- that of those individuals who regularly read as a form of entertainment. However, this is not a group that encompasses only science fiction fandom. There are other genres with their own readership. In addition, the vast majority of science fiction readers are not science fiction fans. At best, this superior trait is a shared trait that is not exclusive to science fiction fandom.

Science fiction fans claim to be scientific literates. The question that must be asked first is, relative to whom? Relative to Christian fundamentalists who believe that the universe is a mere ten thousand years old and that humans and dinosaurs where contemporaries; yes, science fiction fandom does have a greater level of scientific literacy -- and so does most of the general populace. I have heard the worst kind of junk science and pseudo-science spouted from the mouths of science fiction fans over the years and seen much of the same drivel on fan websites. Overall, the scientific literacy of fandom cannot be said to be that much greater than that of the average individual in society.

Now there is a subgroup within fandom, the fans of "hard science" science fiction who do display a high degree of literacy in regards to the physical sciences. Alas, these persons usually tend to be abysmally ignorant of the social sciences, as well as the humanities. They find it to be perfectly realistic that four hundred, two thousand, ten thousand years hence that the social and economic structure of future society will be just the same as it was in the late twentieth century.

Endnote This is not scientific literacy, as far as I'm concerned. To be scientific literate, you should have a basic grounding in both the physical and the social sciences, not just one or the other.

Science fiction fans have a "sense of wonder"... There are so many different definitions of this term within science fiction and science fiction fandom that it is difficult to discuss this supposed superior trait. Regardless, it doesn't matter any more. The term has passed into popular culture, because all of us now experience either a "sense of wonder" or a dread of "the engines of the night" in this world of fast paced technological change. The wonder of brave new worlds, fantastic new technologies, strange sights never before seen, and godlike powers are no longer the private reserve of science fiction readers or of science fiction fandom. It is part of mundane, mainstream culture. When such topics are reported, albeit briefly and poorly, on the tabloid news programmes they cease to be subcultural; they have moved into the cultural. Same goes for the antithesis to the "sense of wonder", "the engines of the night" -- the dark nightmares of the possible abuse and threat that could arise out of these new technlogies and capabilities. Again, this is not a trait exclusive to science fiction fandom.

So, just what is unique about science fiction fandom? Only the false perception that science fiction fans are superior to everybody else. Guess what, they're not.

Endnote:
Yes, the writers do employ the device that things will mostly be the same as they are now and they do it because they are writing fiction. They are trying to tell a story about people in a fantastical setting and they have to use the reference point of contemporary culture. One, because, in most cases, it is the only culture that they truely know. Two, because it is, again in most cases, the only culture that the intended readership really knows. Consider the simple boy-meets-girl tale that is Day Million and imagine how incomprehensible a longer, more complex story would be if it were written in this style. However, there is a big difference between a writer using a literary device to communicate to the reader and a fan believing that a literary device is how the future is going to be.

Back   Table of Contents   Next

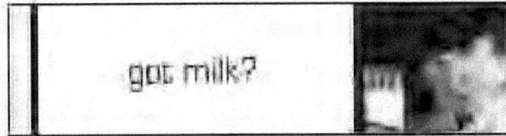

A Brief History of Swill

Back   Table of Contents   Next

It all began as a surreal, last minute, idle prank.

The Catalyst:

I was attending York University in Toronto. My old high school friend, Lester Rainsford, as also at York. Another friend of ours from high school, Andrew Hoyt, was studying at the University of Ottawa. In early October of 1980, I pitched the idea to Lester that we should all attend Maplecon III in Ottawa. I was going to the convention anyway -- some other friends and I were entering the masquerade as droogs from A Clockwork Orange -- and I thought that Lester and Andrew might enjoy attending the convention. Both were science fiction readers, but had never attended a convention nor had any interest in fandom.

When Lester found out that this was going to be a science fiction and comic book convention, he initially had cold feet about attending. Then, he had the idea that we should distribute a boycott flyer at the convention. It told him that that would be pointless, since anybody who would read the flyer would already be attending the convention. His reply was, "Exactly."

So a couple of days before the convention, Lester with my help bashed out the boycott flyer on my aging manual typewriter. The flyer was offensive, outrageously politically incorrect by present standards, with intentional poor grammar, typos, misspellings, and strikeouts. We printed 500 copies and headed off to Ottawa.

At the convention, Andrew and Lester quickly became bored. They found the panels to be dull or stupid, the dealers room to be overpriced and a waste of time, and the art show to be laughable. By Saturday morning they were pretending to be sociology graduate students from the University of Toronto gathering initial research on deviant subcultures -- comic book fandom being highly deviant and science fiction fandom simply deviant. Then Andrew noticed that the boycott flyer was creating a stir.

Initially, we were putting out the flyers in piles of twenty. These disappeared quickly, so we started putting them out in piles of ten. These vanished even faster. Andrew and Lester noticed that everytime some of the boycott flyers were set out, a someone wearing a special coloured badge -- I forget the colour, but it was the colour that indicated that the person was part of the convention committee -- would spirit away the entire pile. And so began a game of cat and mouse.

We started putting out flyers in piles of five, then one. The convention committee eventually stationed somebody to watch the table. Tape was borrowed from the front desk and the flyers were put up in several places on the convention floor and in some of the panel rooms. Now there was some poor sod patrolling the entire convention floor searching for our boycott flyers. At this time, I was getting ready for the masquerade judging. We split the remaining flyers between us, and I headed off to join my droogs.

Lester and Andrew amused themselves getting rid of their remaining flyers. They slipped them in, underneath other flyers, had a small pile set out on the hotel literature and tourist info table, and even had some set out at the hotel bar... When their flyers were gone, they left to go back to Andrew's residence.

After the judging -- the droogs won first prize for best group costume -- I distributed the rest of my flyers at various room parties. The last batch I slipped in on the flyer table before I retired to my hotel room.

Lester and Andrew returned to the convention early Sunday afternoon and we all went to the train station where Lester and I caught the train back to

Toronto. Aside of the fun with the boycott flyer, the convention had been a bust for both Lester and Andrew and I don't think that they have attended any since then.

The Reaction:

Back in Toronto, things were the same as usual until I attended the next monthly fan gathering. Here I heard that the local powers that be -- the Big Name Fans of Toronto -- were looking for who was responsible for the boycott flyer. It appeared that the Ottawa fan organisation that hosted Maplecon was very upset about the flyer and that they held OSFiC responsible. Of course, I found this to be hilarious.

- First that anybody would believe that OSFiC actually wrote the flyer
- Second that anybody would be stupid enough to believe that OSFiC would write the flyer and sign their name to it

I mentioned this to Lester and he suggested that we do something to really annoy the Big Name Fans. And so the germ of Swill was born. Christmas break came and went. When we got back Lester, Andrew, and I began work on the magazine that would become Swill.

The Products:

In February of 1981 the first issue of Swill appeared. I no longer have any copies of the magazine, so I will have to go on recollection alone. It contained an Editorial by myself, columns by Lester and Andrew, some filler, and a reprint of the boycott flyer. I called the publishing company VileFen Press and the magazine had a punk look to it. I think I had 200 copies made and charged one dollar -- or whatever I could get -- for the magazine. At the February fan gathering I brought some copies that I handed out for free.

Well, the proverbial faecal matter struck the fan. All of the Big Name Fans in Toronto were very very angry with me. Of course, in true fannish

14

fashion, nobody said anything directly to me. So, whatever I heard was second or third hand at best. Not that that really mattered. The details were unimportant; the general consensus was that people were angry and disapproved.

Swill was intended as a one-shot, single-issue magazine. However, with the response it received, Lester and I decided that more issues should be produced. Another York student, using the name Stephano, joined as our cartoonist and we set out to produce a second issue. This time, I enlisted the facilities of a friend in Guelph to print the magazine rather than use a printing company. The mimeograph was cheaper and gave Swill that grunge look that so befitted it.

In all, six or seven issues of Swill were published. Of those issues the first four were the best, in particular issues two and three. At the time of issue four was published two things happened that changed Swill and led to its decline.
- I moved to Vancouver
- Stephano began to publish his own version of Swill called BeSwill.

While I was getting settled in Vancouver, Swill ceased to be published.

In Ontario, BeSwill was being published, but BeSwill was... I don't know how to describe it, just weird, a side branch of Swill that was in essence a separate species.

In the late summer of '81 I began to publish Swill again, but it was not the same as the original four issues. I don't remember how many issues I published from Vancouver, two or three, but as the year drew to a close so did Swill. No longer living in Ontario, I had any real desire to try and tick off Toronto fandom. I was getting more and more involved in the anti-arms race peace movement and the anarchist community to spend time on Swill. The drive and the desire had faded. As of February 1982, Swill was no more.

Aftermath:

In 1984 I published three issues of a magazine called Daughter of Swill, Mother of Scum. This magazine had some of the same spirit that was in Swill, but it was also quite different. Each issue was an essay on a single topic; one on fandom and fascism, one on the science fiction of winnable nuclear war, and one on the lack of alien aliens in science fiction. These were distributed to a select group of friends. Of these three issues, the one on science fiction aliens was the best. Again, no known copies of this magazine survive -- and it is probably for the best.

In 1991, I wrote the magazine Scum. It had a series of essays in it on various topics about the genre and one on fandom. Some reprints of old Swill columns, such as Lester Rainsford's rant against Libertarian Party science fiction, "A Gram of Brains, is Worth a Pound of Shit" as well as some material that had been written for Swill by Hoyt and Rainsford, but never published. I wrote Scum, but I never published it. It and all the Swill related things went into a box in the basement. And there it rested until a basement flood some years later reduced it and several other items to garbage.

In 2001, Swill Online was published.

And that is the history of Swill.

Back   Table of Contents   Next

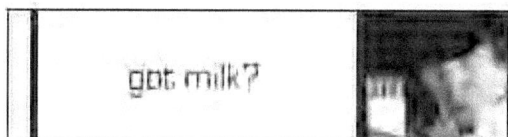

got milk?

EndNotes

Back   Table of Contents   Home

Swill Online is a project that will run from February 22rd, 2001 to January 31st, 2002.

The site will be updated on an irregular basis throughout the year. To any of our old columnists and contributors out there please feel free to send us something new for the site.

Contact Information

Swill Online
swill@klathaentertainment.com

Back   Table of Contents   Next

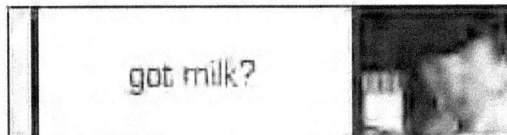
got milk?

CODA

A list of SWILL volumes:

Original SWILL	issues 1 through 7
SWILL 2011	issues 8 through 12
SWILL 2012	issues 13 through 17
SWILL 2013	issues 18 through 22
SWILL 2014	issues 23 through 26
SWILL 2015	issues 27 through 30
SWILL 2016/2017	issues 31 through 35
SWILL Annuals: Volume 1	issues 36 through 40

Vile Fen Press

a division of Klatha Entertainment an Uldune Media company